I0022803

How to Raise Mentally Strong Children With ADHD

100 Practical Strategies Every Parent Can Use to Reduce Stress, Calm Chaos, and Improve Family Life

Talia Rowen

© Copyright 2025 – Talia Rowen – All rights reserved

The content within this book may not be reproduced, duplicated, or transmitted without direct written permission from the author or the publisher.

Under no circumstances will any blame or legal responsibility be held against the publisher, or author, for any damages, reparation, or monetary loss due to the information contained within this book, either directly or indirectly.

Legal Notice

This book is copyright protected. This book is only for personal use. You cannot amend, distribute, sell, use, quote, or paraphrase any part, or the content within this book, without the consent of the author-publisher.

Disclaimer Notice

Please note that the information contained within this document is for educational and entertainment purposes only. All effort has been executed to present accurate, up-to-date, and reliable, complete information. No warranties of any kind are declared or implied. Readers acknowledge that the author is not engaging in the rendering of legal, financial, medical, or professional advice.

Table of Content

About Me and Why I Wrote This Book

O ne evening I found myself sitting on the bathroom floor with my back against the door while my son shouted on the other side. What had started as a simple request to brush his teeth had spiraled into a full-blown battle. I had already raised my voice, he had slammed the door, and both of us were locked in our corners, furious and exhausted. I remember pressing my palms against the cold tiles and thinking, is this what every night will look like from now on? That moment stayed with me, not because it was unusual, but because it was painfully ordinary in our home.

The truth is that many days looked like that. Mornings unraveled before they even began. Someone couldn't find their shoes, someone else forgot a homework assignment, cereal spilled across the counter, and by the time we reached the car the bus had already pulled away. Afternoons carried their own battles: crumpled worksheets, slammed doors, endless reminders that turned into nagging. Evenings ended in shouting matches that left the whole house tense. I went to bed each night replaying my words, my tone, the look on my child's face. I wanted so badly to be the calm and steady parent he needed, and instead I felt like I was losing him one small argument at a time.

I tried everything I could find. Sticker charts that peeled off the wall after a week. Checklists that I carefully designed and then forgot to use. Advice from professionals that sounded polished in theory but collapsed under the weight of our messy reality. Friends told me to "be patient" or "stay consistent," but those phrases meant little when I was standing in the kitchen shouting over the chaos. I felt invisible in my own struggle, caught between guilt for not handling things better and anger that no one seemed to understand how relentless it all was.

And yet, not every day ended in defeat. I remember one morning when I decided to tape a short checklist to the bathroom mirror: wash face, brush teeth, get dressed. I handed my son a marker and told him he could check off each step himself. That day, for the first time in weeks, he finished the routine without a fight. I stood in the doorway watching him proudly tick the last box, and for a moment I felt the tightness in my chest ease. It wasn't a miracle, but it was a glimpse of something better. Those small victories mattered more than I realized.

This book was born out of those two kinds of moments: the nights when I slid down the wall in despair and the mornings when a small change gave us back a smile. What I found missing in so many resources was honesty. Too many books sounded either clinical, as if life could be fixed with theories and charts, or overly cheerful, as if ADHD parenting were just a matter of attitude. I wanted a voice that admitted how hard it gets and still offered practical steps you could actually use the next day.

Writing these pages became my way of speaking the words I needed to hear back then. You will not find perfection here, or promises of easy fixes. What you will find are strategies shaped in real family life, tested in the noise of mornings, the tears of homework, and the exhaustion of late nights. Some came from failures that taught me what not to do, others from experiments that worked just enough to keep going. Each of them carries the same hope: to give you room to breathe and to remind you that you are not alone.

If you see yourself in any of these stories, even a little, then this book is also yours. If you have ever ended a day whispering an apology to your child after they were asleep, if you have ever sat in the car after school drop-off trying to gather yourself before heading to work, if you have ever wondered how other families make it look so effortless, then I am writing to you. We may not share the same details, but we share the same desire: to raise children who feel loved, supported, and strong, even when ADHD makes the path uneven.

If part of my story echoes your own, then let's walk this road together.

— Talia

Introduction

It's 7:30 in the morning, and the house already feels like a storm. Shoes are missing, breakfast sits half-eaten on the table, and someone is crying because the pencil they wanted for school isn't sharpened. You raise your voice to hurry things along, only to feel your chest tighten with stress. By the time you get out the door, your child is upset, you're running late, and everyone is starting the day drained. Nights often don't go much better—endless reminders about homework, drawn-out arguments about bedtime, or fights between siblings that leave the whole family tense.

If this picture feels familiar, you're not alone. Parenting a child with ADHD can feel like carrying a backpack filled with heavy stones, one you can't put down even when you're exhausted. The weight isn't only the daily tasks; it's the constant worry that maybe you're doing it wrong, that other families seem calmer, that your patience runs out more often than you'd like to admit. You love your child deeply, but love doesn't erase the chaos, and it doesn't refill your energy when you're running on empty.

Many parents describe the same hidden thoughts: maybe I'm failing, maybe I don't have what it takes, maybe I'm the only one who feels this overwhelmed. Advice from friends or relatives often makes it worse. "Be consistent." "Stay calm." "Set routines." These words sound reasonable, but without concrete tools, they can feel like another way of saying you're not doing enough. What's missing isn't more reminders—it's clear, practical steps that fit into real family life.

Now picture a different version of that same morning. Clothes are set out the night before. A short checklist is taped to the bathroom mirror, guiding your child through brushing teeth, washing their face, and getting dressed. A timer in the kitchen plays a cheerful song to mark when breakfast is over. You still need to give a few nudges, but instead of shouting, you're pointing to the chart or reminding them of the timer. Ten minutes later, everyone is at the door with backpacks in hand. You even have two minutes to sip your coffee before leaving. The whole family starts the day on steadier ground.

That change doesn't come from luck or from being a perfect parent. It comes from using small, intentional strategies that remove some of the friction from daily life. That's what this book offers. You won't find theories about brain chemistry or long lectures about ADHD. You'll find 100 strategies—short, specific, and realistic—designed to lower stress, calm chaos, and strengthen the bond between you and your child. Each one is meant to be something you can try right away, without needing special tools, endless preparation, or hours you don't have.

Some guides make parenting with ADHD sound simple: just stay positive, set clear expectations, or create structure. Anyone who has lived it knows those ideas fall apart if they aren't translated into real actions. That's why this book takes a different approach. Instead of "establish routines," you'll find, "Lay out tomorrow's clothes on the chair before bed, put shoes by the door, and set the table for breakfast in advance." Instead of "improve communication," you'll find, "Sit at your child's eye level, make one request in five words or fewer, and wait for their attention before speaking." Each strategy is grounded in the small, repeatable actions that make family life more manageable.

The point is not to overhaul everything at once. Trying to change ten habits in a week is a recipe for frustration. What works is starting with one strategy, practicing it consistently for a few days, and noticing the difference it makes. A father once shared that his son's evenings always dissolved into tears during homework. Instead of tackling every subject, he started with a single change: setting a fixed start time of 4:30 every day after a snack. That one adjustment cut the arguments in half. Once it became routine, he added another tool—a visual checklist. Within a month, homework wasn't painless, but it was no longer the daily battlefield it used to be.

Every child with ADHD is unique. Some thrive on visual reminders, others respond better to physical rituals, and others need constant movement built into their day. That's why no single strategy will fit every family in the same way. The goal is not to follow a strict formula but to adapt each idea to your child's age, personality, and preferences. For a five-year-old, a visual schedule might be pictures taped on the wall. For a twelve-year-old, it could be a written list they check off themselves. Both approaches serve the same purpose, but the shape shifts to fit the child.

Along the way, you'll also notice that these strategies are not just for your child. They affect you as well. When mornings run smoother, you start the day calmer. When evenings end with a ritual of connection instead of arguments, you go to bed with less guilt. When you protect even twenty minutes for your own rest or hobbies, your patience stretches farther the next time your child melts down. Taking care of yourself isn't a side note—it's part of the plan. A parent who feels steadier creates a home where strategies can actually take root.

You don't need to be perfect. There will be days when nothing works, when your child refuses, when you lose your patience, when the chart is ignored, the timer is thrown, and the evening still ends in tears. Those days don't erase your progress. They're part of the process. Each time you try again, each time you adjust, each time you notice even a small improvement, you're building something lasting.

Think of a mother who tried a visual schedule for her daughter's bedtime. At first, it was a disaster—her daughter ripped it off the wall and refused to follow it. The mother felt defeated, convinced she had failed again. But she didn't give up. A week later, she reintroduced it with stickers her daughter chose herself. This time, the girl proudly placed a sticker on each step as she completed it. Bedtime didn't become magical, but it became bearable, and the mother realized the strategy wasn't wrong—it just needed adapting. That kind of persistence, paired with flexibility, is what brings results.

Parenting a child with ADHD often feels isolating, as if everyone else's families are calmer and more functional. Behind closed doors, many parents face the same struggles you do. The difference is not who loves their child more or who is stronger. The difference lies in having tools that actually fit real life. This book is meant to put those tools in your hands, one page at a time.

As you move forward, imagine yourself collecting small pieces of stability. One routine that makes mornings easier. One phrase that softens bedtime. One ritual that turns conflict into warmth. One habit that protects your own well-being. None of these alone will transform everything overnight. But together, step by step, they create a home where ADHD is part of the picture without dominating it. They create mornings where you can breathe, evenings where you can smile, and relationships that feel less strained and more connected.

This introduction is not here to convince you that life with ADHD will suddenly be easy. It won't. But it can be lighter, calmer, and more manageable than it feels right now. The way forward isn't through perfection or grand gestures. It's through consistent, practical strategies that you can start today, right where you are, with what you already have.

So take a breath. You don't need to do it all at once. You don't need to fix every problem today. All you need is one step, one strategy, one change that makes tomorrow a little smoother than today. This book will walk with you through those steps, giving you a set of tools to carry—not heavy stones that weigh you down, but small anchors that steady your family as you move forward together.

How to Use This Book

Y ou may feel tempted to race through the pages, searching for that one answer that will make life smoother right away. Slow down. This book isn't designed to overwhelm you with theory or bury you in rules. Think of it as a toolbox. Each chapter is a drawer, and inside are ten tools you can pick up whenever you need them.

The book is divided into ten chapters, each focused on an area of daily life with a child who has ADHD: routines, school, discipline, emotional strength, social skills, communication, health, technology, family relationships, and your own well-being. You don't need to read them in order. If mornings are your biggest battle, turn straight to Chapter 1. If school is the sore spot right now, start with Chapter 2. The idea is to meet your most urgent need before moving on.

Every strategy stands on its own. They're short, specific, and built to be tested in real life. You don't need to master all 100. In fact, trying to do too much at once usually backfires. The best results come when you start small and stay consistent.

Here's how to get the most out of the book:

- **Choose your entry point.** Open the chapter that fits your most urgent challenge. There's no required order.

- **Start small.** Pick one strategy, try it for five to seven days, and watch what changes.

- **Adapt to your child.** A visual chart might be drawings for a five-year-old and a written checklist for a twelve-year-old. The principle is the same, the form can vary.

- **Track progress.** Keep a simple notebook or chart: "Tried the homework timer—five minutes was too short, ten minutes worked better." Notes like these give you clarity and show you wins you might forget.

- **Protect yourself too.** No strategy works if you're running on fumes. Even twenty minutes of real rest can change how you handle a meltdown later.

- **Drop perfection.** A failed attempt isn't proof you're doing it wrong—it's feedback. Adjust and try again.

One father told me his evenings always ended in shouting over homework. Instead of changing everything, he chose one small step: homework began at 4:30 every day after a snack. It seemed too simple, yet within two weeks the yelling had dropped by half. That win gave him the courage to add a checklist, then a timer. Piece by piece, evenings turned from battles into routines.

A mother shared a similar story about bedtime. Her daughter ripped down the first visual schedule she tried. A week later, she reintroduced it with stickers her daughter picked out herself. This time, it worked. What looked like failure was just part of finding the right fit.

This book is meant to walk beside you, not judge you. Open the toolbox, pick one tool, and try it out. Over days and weeks, these small actions add up. They don't erase ADHD, but they make home life calmer, mornings smoother, and evenings softer. That's the kind of change that lasts.

Chapter 1:
Strategies To Build Stress Free Daily Routines

"Children thrive when their world is predictable, and parents thrive when stress does not rule the day." — Ross Greene

I t's 7:15 in the morning. One child can't find their shoes, another is still in pajamas, the kitchen table is covered with half-eaten cereal bowls, and you're already raising your voice for the third time. Backpacks aren't packed, the bus is coming, and someone just remembered a permission slip that was supposed to be signed last night. By the time you get out the door, everyone's heart is racing, tempers are flaring, and you feel like you've already run a marathon before the day has even begun.

Now picture a different version of that same morning. Clothes are laid out, breakfast is simple but ready, your child knows what to do next without being told ten times, and you actually have three minutes to sip your coffee before heading out. No yelling, no last-minute searches, no knots in your stomach. The difference between the two mornings isn't luck—it's routine. Predictable rhythms turn chaos into calm, and when you have a child with ADHD, this difference is even more powerful.

This chapter is about giving you tools to build that calmer version of family life. Not with abstract advice or complicated systems, but with clear, doable strategies you can start using tomorrow. You don't need to overhaul your entire household at once. You just need to create small anchors—predictable steps your child can count on—that guide the day in a smoother direction.

Think of routine like the rails of a train track. Without them, the train wanders off course, stopping wherever distractions pull it. With them, it moves forward with less effort, less conflict, and more confidence. For children with ADHD, those rails don't just help them stay on track; they also lower the daily battles that leave you drained.

I once spoke with a mother named Elena who used to dread weekday mornings. Her son, Matteo, would resist getting dressed, wander off in the middle of brushing his teeth, and melt down when it was time to leave. She felt like every day began with a fight. After putting a few simple routines in place—clothes folded on the chair the night before, a short checklist taped to the bathroom mirror, and a playful timer to keep tasks moving—things shifted. Instead of constant arguing, Matteo began following the routine on his own. Elena told me the real gift wasn't just that they left on time; it was that she and her son could actually smile at each other before school.

That's what these strategies are about: giving you back those small but meaningful moments of peace. In the next pages, you'll find ten practical ways to build daily routines that lower stress for you and your child. Each strategy is specific, tested in real family life, and designed to help mornings, evenings, and everything in between feel less like a battleground.

You won't find theory here. What you'll find are things you can try in your own home: morning checklists, evening shortcuts, playful cues, and flexible plans that hold steady even when real life gets messy. By the end of this chapter, you'll have a toolkit of routines that reduce arguments, save time, and bring back a sense of control. More importantly, you'll see how routine—done in a way that fits your family—can transform not only the flow of your day but also the tone of your relationships.

Strategy 1: Establish A Predictable Morning Routine

Mornings can easily spiral into chaos. Your child gets distracted halfway through brushing teeth, pajamas are still on when it's almost time to leave, and you feel like you've asked the same thing ten times. By the time everyone is out the door, stress levels are already high.

What makes the difference is a routine your child can rely on. A simple, repeatable sequence—wake up, wash, dress, eat, grab backpack, leave—removes the guesswork and cuts down on arguments. If clothes and school items are already set aside, the steps flow even more smoothly.

David, a father of a 7-year-old girl named Lily, was used to shouting through the mornings. Lily would forget tasks or get lost in play, and both of them ended up frustrated. David created a poster with five boxes: brush teeth, get dressed, eat breakfast, pack backpack, put on shoes. Each time Lily completed a step, she placed a sticker on the chart. Within a week, mornings turned calmer. Lily followed the sequence with less resistance, and David no longer felt like a drill sergeant.

You can build the same sense of order with tools that fit your home: a checklist taped to the wall, a series of drawings for younger kids, or a simple whiteboard where tasks are checked off. These small visual reminders reduce the need for constant verbal directions and give your child a clear map of what's next.

The key is to keep it consistent. When your child knows the sequence by heart, mornings shift from unpredictable battles to manageable routines. Start with one clear pattern, stick with it, and let the calm build day by day.

Strategy 2: Prepare The Night Before To Avoid Morning Chaos

The most stressful mornings usually begin the same way: clothes are missing, the kitchen is messy, and everyone is rushing in different directions. By the time you're out the door, you're already drained.

A simple evening routine changes that. Ten minutes the night before can clear the biggest roadblocks—laying out tomorrow's clothes, setting the table for breakfast, and creating a ready-to-go spot near the entrance for jackets and shoes. With these basics handled, the morning flows instead of stalls.

The Garcias, a family of four, used to start every day in a rush. Arguments about what to wear or where the sneakers had gone left everyone frustrated. They made one small shift: each evening, they placed outfits on chairs, set the kitchen table, and put shoes by the door. The change was immediate—less shouting, fewer delays, and a calmer atmosphere from the moment they woke up.

You can build the same rhythm at home. Before bed, take a few minutes to:

- Place clothes where your child can find them.
- Set out breakfast dishes so the table is ready.
- Keep shoes and jackets in one visible spot near the door. These steps don't take long, but together they prevent the frantic searches that fuel morning stress.

Start tonight. Choose just two things—prepare tomorrow's clothes and put shoes by the door. Tomorrow morning you'll feel the difference, and once it becomes habit, evenings will hand you back calmer mornings.

Strategy 3: Use Visual Schedules To Guide Daily Tasks

Children with ADHD often tune out repeated verbal reminders. A chart on the wall or a row of simple images works differently: it gives them a guide they can see and follow without constant prompting. Visual schedules reduce arguments because the instructions are already in front of your child, not coming from your mouth over and over again.

Mia discovered this with her son Alex. She drew a simple sequence on a poster—brush teeth, get dressed, eat breakfast, put on shoes—and hung it in the kitchen. Alex loved moving a clothespin down the list after each task. For the first time, he moved through the morning with minimal reminders. Mia said the biggest relief was not repeating herself a dozen times.

You can create the same tool in whatever style fits your family. Use drawings for younger kids, short written steps for older ones, or print icons you find online. Some families prefer a magnetic whiteboard with movable cards, others use a poster with checkboxes or stickers. The important part is that it stays visible and your child interacts with it, marking progress step by step.

Don't try to cover every routine at once. Start with a short sequence of three to five tasks, keep it simple, and let your child choose at least one detail—like the color of the chart or the stickers used. Their involvement makes them more likely to use it.

Start with one small chart tonight. Place it where your child will see it first thing, and tomorrow you'll notice the difference: the chart does the reminding, your voice gets a rest, and your child takes more ownership of their routine.

Strategy 4: Break Big Tasks Into Small Clear Steps

When you tell a child with ADHD to "get ready" or "clean your room," it sounds huge and unmanageable. Their brain struggles to hold all the pieces at once, and that pressure often turns into resistance or delay.

Breaking the task into smaller steps changes the experience. One instruction at a time gives your child something concrete to do, without the weight of the bigger job. Each finished step builds momentum toward the next.

Sophie, a mother of two, discovered this during the morning rush. Every day she would say "Ethan, get ready for school," and every day it ended in conflict. She switched to short, clear prompts: "Put on your socks... now your pants... now your shirt." The same routine suddenly felt doable, and Ethan started moving through it without a fight.

You can apply the same approach to many situations. Instead of "clean your room," say: "Pick up the clothes. Now put the toys in the box. Next, stack the books." Instead of "get ready for bed," try: "Change into pajamas. Brush teeth. Pick a book." Writing a short list can help as a reminder, but the key is guiding your child one step at a time.

Try it today: choose one task your child usually avoids, and instead of giving the full command, break it into three small steps and say them one by one. You'll see how a mountain turns into something they can actually climb.

Strategy 5: Set Up Timers And Alarms As Neutral Reminders

Few things spark tension faster than constant nagging. "Hurry up, brush your teeth!" or "You're running late again!" turns into a power struggle. Children with ADHD, in particular, often push back when reminders come from a parent's voice.

A timer or alarm changes the dynamic. The signal comes from an outside source, not from you, which removes the feeling of being bossed around. The task becomes a response to the beep, the song, or the flashing light—something neutral, almost like a game.

One mother, Karen, used to struggle every evening with her son over bedtime. He would stall endlessly, and she found herself repeating "time to get ready" over and over. She introduced a small visual timer with colored sections that slowly disappeared as minutes passed. When the red portion was gone, it was time to brush teeth and put on pajamas. To her surprise, he accepted the timer's signal without a fight, where before he would argue every night.

There are many ways to make this work. A simple kitchen timer can count down toothbrushing time. A musical alarm on a smart speaker can signal when it's time to put on shoes. A visual timer with moving colors helps children who need to "see" time passing. Pick one or two tools, keep them consistent, and let the device—not your voice—be the reminder.

Try it tonight: set a timer for just one routine, like brushing teeth or ending play. When the beep or song goes off, step back and let the timer "speak." You'll notice less resistance, fewer arguments, and a smoother transition to the next activity.

Strategy 6: Give Choices To Increase Cooperation

When children with ADHD feel cornered by orders, their instinct is often to resist. "Put on your pajamas now" can spark a battle, not because the request is unreasonable, but because the child feels they have no control.

Offering limited choices reduces that resistance. Instead of an open-ended decision that overwhelms, or a rigid command that fuels defiance, you present two acceptable options. The child still has to cooperate, but in a way that preserves a sense of control.

The Ramirez family began using this approach during bedtime struggles. Their son would argue endlessly about getting ready for bed. Instead of repeating, "Brush your teeth now," his mother asked, "Do you want to brush your teeth first or put on pajamas first?" Both options led to bedtime, but the question gave him ownership. With two good choices, the arguments shrank.

You can apply the same method at home in many situations. Offer choices that are simple and both acceptable to you: "Do you want the red cup or the blue cup?" "Do you want to sit on this chair or that one?" Keep it limited to two options, otherwise it becomes confusing. The key is that the outcome is guided by you, but the child feels involved.

Two good choices reduce one big fight. At home, this strategy helps children cooperate without turning every request into a power struggle.

Strategy 7: Use Rewards And Praise To Reinforce Routine Success

Even when routines are clear, children with ADHD may need an extra spark to keep them going. Without recognition, the effort behind small steps can fade, and routines slip back into arguments. A touch of praise or a visible marker of success helps your child see progress and feel proud of it.

One mother, Rachel, used a simple sticker chart during the morning rush. Each time her son finished a step without stalling—getting dressed, brushing teeth, putting on shoes—he added a sticker. After collecting five stickers, he chose the breakfast cereal for Saturday. The chart turned mornings from a shouting match into a smoother process, because her son could see his progress building day by day.

You can do the same in your home. Choose one routine—morning or evening—and create a chart with two or three steps. Each time your child completes a step, let them add a sticker, a checkmark, or even draw a smiley face. Pair it with short, specific praise: "You put your shoes on right away, that was quick thinking." Keep the rewards immediate and small so the connection is clear.

Save this tool for home routines only. When mornings and evenings move more smoothly, the whole family feels the difference.

Strategy 8: Keep Routines Flexible Enough For Real Life

Routines bring calm, but if they're too rigid, they can backfire. Life happens—traffic makes you late, breakfast spills, or your child wakes up slower than usual. When every minute is locked in stone, small disruptions create big stress.

Flexibility keeps the structure working. Allowing a few minutes of wiggle room or having a backup plan helps your child adapt without throwing the whole morning off track. The goal is rhythm, not perfection.

Take the Johnson family. They used to panic if their son wasn't dressed exactly on time. Arguments would erupt, and mornings ended in tears. Then they built in a five-minute cushion and agreed that, if breakfast ran late, a granola bar in the car was an acceptable backup. The fights disappeared, and the routine held together even on rough days.

You can apply the same mindset. Keep your routine consistent, but allow small adjustments: add a margin of time, swap one step when needed, or carry breakfast to go if necessary. The key is to protect the sequence while giving it enough room to bend.

Keep this flexibility for morning and evening routines at home—those small cushions prevent daily stress without breaking the structure.

Strategy 9: Involve Your Child In Creating The Routine

When routines are imposed from above, children often resist. They feel controlled, and pushback becomes part of the daily struggle. For kids with ADHD, having no say in the process makes cooperation even harder.

Involving your child changes the dynamic. When they help design the routine, they feel ownership. That sense of "this is my plan too" increases motivation and reduces conflict.

For example, Laura invited her daughter Mia to help with the evening routine. Instead of dictating the order, she asked, "Do you want to brush your teeth before or after putting on pajamas?" Mia chose the order herself and proudly drew little pictures for each step on a poster. Once she felt the routine was partly hers, she followed it with far less resistance.

You can try this in simple ways. Let your child choose between two acceptable options (pajamas first or teeth first). Ask them to decorate the checklist with drawings or stickers. Older kids can write out the steps themselves or suggest the order. The more they feel included, the more they'll stick with it.

Keep these choices within daily home routines—when children shape the order at home, they cooperate more and resist less.

Strategy 10: Review And Adjust Routines As Children Grow

The routines that work today won't always fit tomorrow. As children grow, their needs, schedules, and energy levels change. A routine that once kept things smooth can suddenly feel outdated or too restrictive.

Reviewing and adjusting routines prevents frustration. Every few months, take a step back and notice: Is bedtime still realistic? Has morning prep become longer because of new activities? Small updates keep the structure relevant and effective.

Take Daniel, who started middle school this year. His old evening routine ended at 8:30 p.m., but homework and sports meant he wasn't ready for bed until later. His parents adjusted by moving lights-out to 9:15 and adding ten minutes of quiet reading before sleep. The new routine matched his age and responsibilities, and bedtime arguments eased.

You can do the same in your home. Revisit your child's routines every three to six months. Ask yourself: do the steps still make sense? Does the timing fit their current schedule? Involve your child in small decisions, but keep the structure steady. Updating doesn't mean starting from scratch—it means fine-tuning what already works.

Keep these reviews focused only on daily home routines—mornings, evenings, meals, and bedtime—not schoolwork or outside activities. When routines grow with your child, they remain useful tools instead of battles to fight.

Chapter 2:
Strategies To Support School Success At Home And In Class

"Every child can learn, just not in the same way or on the same day." — George Evans

I t's a Tuesday afternoon, and your child has just come home from school. The backpack is half-zipped, papers are crumpled at the bottom, and a math worksheet is already missing. When it's time to start homework, he fidgets in his chair, gets up for a snack, and insists he can't find a pencil. Later that evening, an email arrives from the teacher: "Forgot assignment again." You sigh, feeling like school is an uphill battle that never ends.

The next day isn't much better. During class, he blurts out answers without raising his hand, forgets to turn in work he actually finished, and ends up with another note sent home. By the time you read it, you're torn between frustration and worry. You know your child is bright and capable, but the daily cycle of missing assignments, constant reminders, and classroom struggles leaves everyone exhausted.

Now imagine a different picture. Homework begins at a set time after a short break, not after an hour of arguing. Assignments are written in a planner and checked off one by one. The backpack is packed the same way every evening, so mornings don't begin with frantic searches. Notes from the teacher aren't surprises anymore but part of a simple daily communication system. School hasn't turned into an easy ride, but the constant chaos has been replaced by a rhythm that feels manageable.

I think of James, an eight-year-old whose parents dreaded homework time. He would stall for nearly an hour, melting down before ever writing a word. Once his family introduced a fixed start time, short breaks, and a clear checklist, the nightly battles eased. James still needed support, but instead of frustration and tears, homework became a series of steps he could complete. His parents described it as "the difference between chaos and progress."

Another mother, Carla, faced a different problem. Her daughter Sofia often forgot to bring home the right books, and every week she received notes from the teacher about missing work. Carla and Sofia began using a simple daily planner and a communication sheet signed by both teacher and parent. Within weeks, the pile of missing assignments shrank, and the notes home became less about problems and more about small successes.

These examples show what many parents discover: children with ADHD don't need more lectures or pressure. They need strategies that turn vague expectations into clear, repeatable steps. With the right tools, challenges like homework battles, forgotten supplies, and classroom difficulties become less overwhelming and more predictable.

This chapter will give you ten practical strategies that you can apply both at home and in partnership with your child's teachers. You'll learn how to set a consistent homework start time, create a quiet workspace, use checklists to track assignments, and build daily systems of communication. We'll also cover ways to teach your child to pack their backpack, encourage effort over results, and coordinate with school for extra support.

These strategies won't erase every difficulty, but they will give your child a stronger foundation for success. And just as important, they will help you step out of the endless cycle of nagging, searching, and worrying. With clear routines and cooperative systems in place, school can become less of a battlefield and more of a place where progress, big or small, actually feels possible.

Strategy 1: Create A Homework Routine With A Fixed Start Time

Homework often turns into a battlefield when the start time is left open. Children with ADHD are experts at delaying what feels difficult. A vague "we'll start later" quickly becomes "not now" and then "too late." Without a clear starting point, the evening slips away and homework becomes a source of stress for everyone.

A fixed start time changes the tone. When the rule is clear, your child knows when work begins and no longer feels like it is up for debate. The best approach is to place homework after a short reset that is only meant to prepare for study, such as a snack, a bathroom break, or ten minutes of light play. This limited pause helps your child release energy before shifting into schoolwork, without becoming part of the wider household routine.

The Rivera family tried this after months of nightly arguments. Their son Daniel always promised he would start "in a few minutes," but those minutes stretched into an hour of wandering around the house. They set a simple rule: homework would always start at 4:30, right after his snack and a short stretch in the yard. At first Daniel pushed back, but the consistency paid off. Within two weeks, he no longer argued about starting. Everyone in the family knew that at 4:30, homework began, and the stress around schoolwork dropped dramatically.

You can create the same structure at home. Pick a realistic time that works for your family's schedule. Make it clear that this time does not change from day to day. Use a timer or a simple reminder so the start is not negotiable. If your child asks for "five more minutes," you can point to the clock instead of entering another argument.

When homework starts at the same time every day, it stops being a fight and becomes part of school life.

Strategy 2: Break Homework Into Short Work Periods With Breaks

Long homework sessions can feel endless for children with ADHD. Even when they sit down with the best intentions, attention fades quickly and frustration takes over. Asking them to stay focused for an hour almost guarantees arguments, wandering, or tears.

Breaking the work into short periods with planned pauses makes study time more manageable. A clear cycle of fifteen to twenty minutes of focus followed by a short reset helps your child stay engaged without burning out. These breaks are not rewards, but built-in parts of the system that refresh body and mind before the next round of work.

The Harris family used this approach with their daughter Zoe. Homework time often ended in slammed doors and unfinished pages. They introduced a simple system: twenty minutes of math or reading, then five minutes to stretch, drink water, or move around the room. A timer signaled each switch. Knowing she only had to concentrate for a short stretch changed Zoe's mindset. The meltdowns decreased, and more work actually got done.

You can apply the same cycle at home. Choose a realistic block of time—fifteen or twenty minutes—then follow it with a short active break. Encourage light movement: a stretch, a few steps around the table, or a sip of water. Reset the timer and start the next work block. Adjust the number of cycles to fit your child's age and workload.

When homework is divided into clear chunks, the task stops feeling overwhelming. Progress appears one block at a time, and resistance gives way to steady effort.

Strategy 3: Use A Quiet And Organized Homework Space

For many children with ADHD, the hardest part of homework isn't the subject itself but the distractions around them. Noise from siblings, toys in view, or a television in the background make focus almost impossible.

A dedicated homework space filters out those distractions. It doesn't need to be elaborate or in a separate room, but it must be consistent, quiet, and clearly designated for schoolwork only. The goal is not to organize the whole house—just to create one spot where your child knows learning happens.

The Miller family set up a simple "homework station" for their son Josh. They cleared a small desk and stocked it only with essentials: sharpened pencils, erasers, a math notebook, and his assignment folder. A lamp gave good lighting, and toys were kept out of sight. At first Josh resisted leaving the living room, but within a week, his focus improved and assignments were finished faster because the space sent a clear signal: this is where schoolwork gets done.

You can do the same at home. Choose a spot—a desk, a corner of the dining table, or a small table in the bedroom—that will always serve as the homework station. Keep only school supplies on it: pencils, ruler, notebook, paper, and the homework folder. Remove distractions such as phones, video games, and unrelated clutter. The consistency of this setup tells your child, every day, that it's time for learning, not play.

The right environment makes focus possible. A quiet, organized homework station helps children with ADHD separate schoolwork from the rest of home life and gives them a clear signal to settle down and start working.

Strategy 4: Use Checklists And Planners To Track Assignments

One of the biggest challenges for children with ADHD is remembering what needs to be done for school. A math worksheet may be buried in the folder, a reading log half-finished, and a spelling list due the next day—but without a clear system, assignments slip through the cracks. These forgotten tasks create frustration at home and negative feedback from teachers.

A checklist or planner keeps schoolwork visible and organized. When tasks are written down and checked off, your child sees progress instead of confusion. The list becomes a daily guide that reduces anxiety and provides a concrete sense of accomplishment.

For example, Noah's parents noticed he frequently forgot small but important tasks, such as turning in a signed form or completing a short reading log. They introduced a simple daily checklist on a whiteboard: math worksheet, reading log, spelling practice, return signed form. Every time Noah completed one, he checked it off. By the end of the week, there were fewer forgotten assignments, and Noah felt proud to see the row of checkmarks as proof of his effort.

You can build the same habit in your home. Some children prefer paper planners with subject boxes, others respond better to a printed sheet or a notebook with one line per assignment. Keep the list specific—"Finish math worksheet" is clearer than "Do homework." Review it together at the start and end of homework time so your child links effort with visible progress.

Each checkmark shows your child that schoolwork is moving forward, one clear step at a time.

Strategy 5: Communicate Daily With Teachers Using A Simple System

One of the biggest frustrations for parents of children with ADHD is discovering problems too late. A missing assignment, an unfinished project, or a behavior issue often comes home as a surprise. Without regular feedback, you feel like you are always reacting instead of staying ahead.

A simple daily communication system prevents this. Unlike the checklist used at home to track homework, this tool is designed only for teacher–parent updates. The goal is not long reports, but short, easy-to-use notes that travel back and forth each day.

The Johnson family set up a "done/not done" sheet with their son's teacher. Every afternoon, the teacher quickly marked whether homework was turned in, behavior was on track, and materials were brought to class. At home, the parents signed the sheet and returned it in the backpack the next day. This two-minute system kept everyone on the same page and cut down on surprise emails about missing work.

You can set this up in different ways depending on what works best with your child's school. Some families use a daily folder that travels back and forth. Others rely on a quick email checklist, or an app if the school provides one. Keep it simple: one page, one checklist, or a few boxes to tick. The system should be easy for teachers to use so it becomes a reliable routine.

A daily system turns school updates into a steady routine, so parents aren't left guessing about homework or behavior.

Strategy 6: Teach Your Child To Pack The Backpack The Same Way Every Day

Forgotten books, missing folders, or a pencil case left at home can turn an ordinary school day into a struggle. For children with ADHD, remembering all the materials they need is one of the biggest daily challenges, and it often leads to frustration both at home and in class.

A backpack routine removes that guesswork. By packing the same way every day, your child develops a predictable system for school materials. The focus here is not on bedtime routines or household chores, but only on preparing the backpack for the next school day.

The Martinez family created a "backpack station" near the front door. On a small shelf, they kept a checklist of items: math notebook, assignment folder, pencil case, water bottle, and snack. Each night, their son checked off the list while placing each item in his backpack. Within a few weeks, he went from constant morning panics to arriving at school with everything he needed.

You can create the same system in your home. Choose a consistent spot where the backpack is always placed. Post a short checklist nearby that includes only school essentials: homework folder, books for the next day, pencil case, and water bottle. Go through it together in the evening until your child learns the sequence. The repetition builds independence and reduces the risk of forgotten items.

A backpack routine keeps school days running smoothly. When the materials are always packed the same way, mornings are calmer, and your child enters the classroom ready to learn.

Strategy 7: Use Positive Reinforcement For School Effort Not Only Results

Children with ADHD often hear more corrections than encouragement. At school this might mean constant reminders about missing homework, forgetting materials, or rushing through assignments. When recognition comes only after a high grade, many children begin to feel that trying is pointless and their motivation drops.

Shifting the focus to effort changes the picture. When you notice and name the steps your child takes, such as starting homework without delay, remembering to bring the right book home, or finishing a reading log, you show them that the process matters, not only the

31

outcome. That recognition makes it easier for them to keep showing up, even when the work feels difficult.

Michael, a ten-year-old, often stalled before math homework. One evening, instead of pointing out how slowly he was moving, his mother said, "I love how you opened your math book right away tonight." His face lit up, and he stayed with the assignment longer than usual. Another parent praised her daughter for packing her backpack the night before, saying, "You remembered everything for tomorrow. That is great preparation." These small acknowledgments gave both children the confidence to try again the next day.

You can do the same by looking for moments to recognize effort in school-related tasks. Keep your words specific: "You started your reading log as soon as we sat down," or "You checked your planner and finished every assignment." Pair the praise with a small gesture such as a smile, a high five, or a pat on the back. No charts or long-term rewards are needed; the immediate recognition is what makes the effort visible.

When effort in schoolwork is noticed consistently, children learn that trying is worthwhile. And when effort feels worthwhile, good habits begin to take root.

Strategy 8: Coordinate With The School For Extra Time And Support

Many children with ADHD can grasp concepts but struggle to show what they know within rigid time limits or long assignments. A timed test may end with half the answers blank, not because your child did not understand, but because their pace is different. Without the right support, these moments chip away at confidence and motivation.

Coordinating with teachers to request extra time or adjusted expectations can make a real difference. Extra minutes on a test, fewer repetitive problems on a worksheet, or a modified assignment allow your child to demonstrate their skills without being set up for failure. These supports are not favors; they are tools that level the playing field.

For example, Marcus often froze during spelling tests. By the time he wrote the first five words, the rest of the class had already finished. After his parents spoke with the teacher, Marcus was given ten extra minutes. With that small change, he was able to complete the list, and his scores began reflecting what he actually knew.

You can advocate for the same adjustments. Start by talking with your child's teacher about specific challenges: Do they need extra time during tests? Reduced homework load? Modified instructions? Keep the discussion practical and collaborative. These are not strategies for home study routines, but formal accommodations agreed upon with the school.

These adjustments don't lower expectations—they give your child a fair chance to demonstrate what they actually know.

Strategy 9: Encourage Active Learning Methods At Home

Traditional homework often expects children to sit still and copy information, but this approach rarely works well for kids with ADHD. Long stretches of passive work drain their focus and create frustration. They learn more effectively when movement and multisensory activities are built into the study process.

Active learning turns assignments into something the body and mind do together. Reading words out loud while walking, spelling while bouncing a ball, or using coins to solve math problems makes the work more engaging and easier to retain. These activities are not physical exercise for health; they are tools to help your child process and remember school material.

Take Sarah, a nine-year-old who dreaded spelling lists. Her father turned practice into a movement game: for each word, Sarah hopped once as she spelled each letter. Instead of groaning, she laughed her way through the list and remembered more words the next day at school.

You can adapt this method to different subjects. Use flashcards while pacing around the room, place math problems on sticky notes along a wall and solve them one by one, or act out vocabulary words to reinforce meaning. Keep sessions short and connected directly to the homework task, so the activity boosts attention without turning into general playtime.

Movement should be part of homework time, not a replacement for physical exercise. When used this way, it keeps your child engaged with schoolwork and makes learning feel more achievable.

Strategy 10: Review Progress Weekly And Celebrate Small Wins

Homework and school routines often feel like an endless grind, especially when progress comes in tiny steps. Without pausing to notice what is working, both you and your child may only see the struggles. That constant sense of falling short drains motivation for the week ahead.

A short weekly review changes the picture. By setting aside a fixed moment—such as Sunday evening—you and your child can look back at what was completed and highlight small successes. This is not a time for criticism or pointing out mistakes, but a chance to notice effort and progress.

For example, the Reynolds family started a ten-minute check-in every Friday night. Together they reviewed homework folders and planners. When their daughter Emma saw that she had turned in all her reading logs that week, she felt proud. The family marked the win with a simple celebration connected only to school: choosing a movie as a reward for completed assignments. That recognition gave Emma energy to keep trying the following week.

You can do the same in your home. Pick one regular time each week, look at assignments that were finished, and highlight at least one success. Pair the review with a small ritual tied directly to school progress, such as choosing a fun activity when all homework is turned in. Keep the focus strictly on academic work, not on general family bonding or household routines.

Weekly check-ins keep motivation alive when they stay centered on schoolwork. By limiting the review to homework and assignments, you give your child a clear message: effort in learning is noticed, valued, and worth celebrating.

Chapter 3:
Strategies To Use Positive Discipline And Manage Behavior

"Discipline is not about control, it is about teaching children how to control themselves." — Daniel J. Siegel

T he shouting has already started. Your child is on the floor, kicking and screaming because a sibling touched their toy. You try to intervene, but within seconds you are yelling too, threatening punishments you don't really believe in. The noise fills the house, and when it finally quiets down, no one feels better. Your child is still upset, you are exhausted, and nothing has been learned for next time.

Many parents of children with ADHD know this cycle well. Traditional discipline—yelling, punishments, or threats—often brings only short-term compliance. In fact, it can escalate defiance, damage trust, and leave both you and your child feeling stuck in the same exhausting pattern. These methods might stop the behavior in the moment, but they rarely teach children how to manage themselves in the long run.

Now picture a different scene. Your child ignores the request to turn off the TV, but instead of shouting, you walk over, switch it off calmly, and say, "Screen time is over. You can try again tomorrow if you follow the rule tonight." There is some grumbling, but no explosion. The boundary is clear, the consequence is consistent, and you keep your calm. Over time, your child learns that rules are predictable and that losing a privilege for a short time is the result of a choice they made, not of your anger.

That contrast captures the heart of this chapter. Children with ADHD often test limits more intensely, react more strongly to frustration, and struggle with self-control. Harsh punishments, though tempting in moments of stress, usually make things worse. What they need is guidance that is firm but fair, consistent but compassionate. Positive discipline does not mean letting misbehavior slide. It means using tools that teach responsibility, build self-control, and keep the parent-child relationship intact.

I think of Daniel, a seven-year-old whose parents used to send him to his room for every meltdown. He would slam the door, scream for half an hour, and come out angrier than before. When his parents shifted to a different approach—staying nearby, helping him calm down, and setting clear but reasonable limits—the fights slowly lost their intensity. Daniel still had outbursts, but they ended faster, and he began learning how to bring himself back under control. His parents said the real breakthrough was realizing that discipline was not about "winning the battle" but about teaching Daniel what to do the next time he felt overwhelmed.

This chapter will give you ten strategies to manage behavior with that same perspective. You will learn how to set clear and simple rules, respond with consistent consequences, stay calm in the middle of conflict, and use methods like "time in" or calm-down spaces instead of isolating punishments. You will see how praising good behavior early, offering structured choices, and modeling respect can change the atmosphere at home.

The goal is not perfection or instant obedience. The goal is to build skills in your child that last: self-control, respect for others, and the ability to handle frustration without spiraling into chaos. Along the way, you will also protect your own energy, because discipline becomes less about endless fights and more about steady guidance.

With these strategies, you can move away from the cycle of yelling and punishing and toward a calmer, more constructive way of shaping behavior. Positive discipline is not about controlling your child; it is about helping them learn to control themselves.

Strategy 1: Set Clear And Simple Rules For Behavior

Children with ADHD often feel lost when rules are vague or too many. Endless reminders like "Don't shout, don't run, don't argue" blur together, and nothing sticks.

A short set of clear rules works better. Limiting expectations to three to five makes them easier to remember and apply. The goal is not to cover every possible behavior but to highlight the basics that make home life respectful and safe.

The Parker family tried this after years of constant nagging. They chose three house rules and wrote them on a poster: "Use kind words. Keep hands to yourself. Listen the first time." Whenever conflicts arose, the parents pointed to the poster instead of repeating lectures. Over time, their children began to use the rules themselves, and fights at home decreased.

You can do the same. Pick the behaviors that matter most in your family—kind words, safe hands, respectful listening—and write them in short, positive language. Post the rules where everyone can see them, such as on the fridge or a bedroom wall. This makes expectations predictable and easy to reference in moments of tension.

Clear, visible rules guide behavior at home and keep family life calmer.

Strategy 2: Use Consistent Consequences Without Harsh Punishment

When a child with ADHD misbehaves, parents often feel the urge to raise their voice or threaten severe punishments. Yelling or spanking might stop the behavior in the moment, but it rarely teaches lasting lessons. Harsh punishments often fuel anger, shame, and more defiance.

Consistent and proportionate consequences work better. Instead of punishing out of frustration, you decide in advance what the outcome will be for certain behaviors and follow through calmly every time. The consequence should be short, clear, and directly connected to what happened.

For example, when eight-year-old Lucas threw a toy across the room, his parents didn't yell or ban all toys for a week. They calmly told him, "Throwing toys is not safe. This toy is taking a 15-minute break." When his sister was shouted at during play, the rule was the same: "If you can't use respectful words, you take a short break from the game." Over time, Lucas understood that each action led to the same, predictable result.

You can apply the same principle at home. If a toy is misused, the toy takes a break. If a child is rough with a sibling, the playtime pauses. Keep the consequence short and directly tied to the behavior so that the lesson is clear. The consistency matters more than the length or severity.

In the home setting, calm and predictable consequences show children that discipline is about safety and respect, not fear.

Strategy 3: Stay Calm And Neutral During Conflicts

Children with ADHD often test limits with shouting, refusal, or hurtful words. In those moments, it is natural for parents to feel provoked and to respond emotionally. But when tempers rise on both sides, conflicts escalate instead of resolving.

Staying calm and neutral makes discipline more effective. A steady voice and composed body language prevent the situation from spiraling further. The goal here is not to have a deep conversation but to show that rules still apply, even when emotions run high.

For example, nine-year-old Emma once yelled at her mother, "I hate you!" Instead of shouting back, her mother kept her tone neutral and said, "I hear that you are upset. We will talk when you are calm." Emma stormed off, and the fight ended quickly. Later, when Emma had calmed down, her mother reminded her of the house rule about respectful words. She also explained that if the same language was used again, Emma would lose ten minutes of playtime with her tablet. The message was clear: staying calm does not mean ignoring disrespect, it means handling it without adding fuel to the fire.

You can practice this by focusing on your own response first. Lower your voice instead of raising it. Keep your words short and steady, such as "We'll talk after you calm down." Take a slow breath before answering, and use neutral body language—standing tall, avoiding finger-pointing, and keeping your face relaxed. These signals tell your child that you are in control, even if they are not.

In discipline moments, staying calm keeps the power struggle from escalating and shows children that respect is expected, even when emotions run high.

Strategy 4: Use Time In Instead Of Time Out

Many parents resort to "time out" when a child loses control. The child is sent away to their room or a chair in isolation, often left crying or screaming until the clock runs out. For children with ADHD, this often backfires. They come back angrier, feeling rejected rather than calmer or more prepared to behave differently.

A "time in" works differently. Instead of isolating your child, you stay nearby and guide them toward regaining control. This is not about having a deep emotional talk—it is about handling misbehavior with calm presence while teaching that every action has limits. The child learns that even when they lose control, discipline means correction, not abandonment.

Consider six-year-old Ben. Whenever he hit his sister, his parents used to send him to his room. He would slam the door, yell for twenty minutes, and come out still furious. They decided to try "time in" instead. The next time Ben lashed out, his father brought him to the couch, sat beside him, and said calmly, "You need a break. Sit here with me until your body is calm." They breathed together and waited. When Ben settled, his father reminded him of the house rule about safe hands and explained that if hitting happened again, he would lose ten minutes of playtime. Ben apologized and returned to play. The lesson was not just calm—it was the clear link between behavior, pause, and consequence.

You can use this at home by choosing a calm spot like a couch or a chair in a quiet corner. When your child loses control, bring them there and stay close. Keep your words short: "We're sitting here until you're calm." Once the storm passes, restate the rule and, if necessary, outline the consequence for repeating the behavior.

Time in works when it teaches children that misbehavior has a pause and correction, but never rejection.

Strategy 5: Catch And Praise Good Behavior Early

Children with ADHD often hear feedback only when something goes wrong. The toy is grabbed too quickly, the voice is raised too loud, or the rules are forgotten. What gets overlooked are the small moments when your child does exactly what you hope for. If those moments pass in silence, the message they receive is that good behavior is invisible, while mistakes always stand out.

Catching positive behavior right when it happens changes that pattern. Immediate praise tells your child, "I saw that, and it matters." The sooner you notice, the stronger the link becomes between the action and the recognition. Over time, this makes it far more likely that the behavior will be repeated.

One evening, a father was playing a board game with his children. His son, who usually shouted over his sister, waited quietly for his turn. The father leaned in and said, "I love how you waited patiently. That made the game more fun for everyone." His son grinned and carried that patience into the next round. The comment took only seconds, but it shaped the rest of the game.

You can apply the same principle in everyday family life:

- Praise your child for using kind words with a sibling.

- Notice when they share a toy without being asked.

- Point out when they calm themselves instead of reacting.

What matters most is that the feedback comes immediately and is tied to a specific action. A quick "I like how you asked politely" or "That was thoughtful when you let your sister go first" is enough to reinforce the moment.

When you make a habit of catching good behavior early, your child learns that positive choices bring attention too, not just mistakes. That awareness motivates them to repeat the behavior and builds a more encouraging atmosphere at home.

Notice the good before correcting the bad.

Strategy 6: Give Choices To Increase Cooperation

When children with ADHD feel cornered by orders, resistance comes fast. A direct "Put on your shoes now" can spark an argument, not because the request is unreasonable, but because the child feels stripped of control.

Offering two clear options lowers that tension. The child still needs to cooperate, but they do so in a way that preserves a sense of choice. The decision is limited, the outcome is guided by you, yet the child experiences ownership of the action.

One morning, a father struggled to get his son dressed for school. Instead of repeating "Hurry up and get ready," he asked, "Do you want to put on your shirt first or your pants first?" Both paths led to the same goal, but the question gave the boy agency. He chose, moved ahead without arguing, and the conflict evaporated.

You can use the same method in many household moments:

- "Do you want the red cup or the blue cup?"

- "Do you want to sit on this chair or that one?"

- "Do you want to read the short story or the comic before lights out?"

Keep it to two choices only, otherwise it becomes confusing. The key is that you remain in charge of the options, while your child feels involved in the process.

Two small choices are often enough to prevent one big fight. In everyday home life, this approach turns ordinary requests into cooperative actions instead of power struggles.

Strategy 7: Use Natural Consequences To Teach Responsibility

Parents often feel pressure to invent punishments when a child misbehaves. But many times, the most powerful lesson comes directly from reality. For children with ADHD, natural consequences are often easier to understand than long explanations or delayed punishments.

Natural consequences mean letting the real outcome of an action teach the lesson. If a toy is left outside, it might get wet. If a child refuses to wear a jacket, they feel cold. These experiences show the link between choice and result more clearly than any lecture.

The Lopez family applied this with their son. He repeatedly left his bike in the yard despite reminders. Instead of scolding again, his parents simply let the bike stay outside. When it rained, the seat was soaked and uncomfortable to ride. Their son quickly understood that leaving the bike out had a cost, and he started parking it in the garage on his own. No yelling, no punishments—just reality doing the teaching.

You can use this approach in your home too. Let your child experience the safe, natural result of their actions instead of rushing to rescue them or adding unrelated punishments. Make sure the consequence is not harmful, only instructive. Over time, these small lessons build real responsibility.

Reality is often the best teacher. At home, natural consequences show children that their choices matter and that responsibility grows from everyday experiences.

Strategy 8: Use Clear And Short Commands

Children with ADHD can quickly lose focus when instructions are long or filled with extra words. A sentence like, "Get ready, we're leaving soon so please put your shoes on quickly" may sound clear to you, but to your child it is overwhelming. Too many words blur the real request, and the chance of resistance grows.

Short, direct commands work better. Two or three words are enough to tell your child exactly what needs to happen. The simpler the message, the easier it is to follow.

The Nguyen family tested this with their son during the morning rush. Instead of saying, "We're going to be late, please stop playing and put on your shoes now," his father simply said, "Shoes on." His son looked up, understood, and complied. The short command cut through distractions and reduced arguments.

You can do the same at home. Replace long sentences with short, clear prompts: "Lights off," "Hands washed," "Table set." Use a calm but firm tone, and be consistent. Avoid adding explanations in the moment—those can come later if needed. The goal during the command is clarity, not conversation.

The shorter the command, the clearer the action. At home, brief instructions help children with ADHD know exactly what is expected without confusion or conflict.

Strategy 9: Use Calm Down Corners Not Punishment Corners

Traditional punishment corners often backfire for children with ADHD. Sitting alone in isolation fuels anger and shame instead of teaching self-control. What helps more is a calm space where your child can settle down and regain balance.

A calm corner is not about discipline. It is a safe spot prepared with items that soothe and comfort. The message is simple: everyone sometimes needs a place to pause and reset.

The Harris family created one in their living room. They placed a beanbag chair, a basket with a stress ball and a few picture books, and added soft lighting. At first they guided their daughter there after intense outbursts. Over time, she began choosing it herself whenever emotions grew too strong. Instead of arguments escalating, she had a constructive way to recover and rejoin family life.

You can create something similar with just a few items. Pick a quiet corner of the house and add cushions, a favorite stuffed toy, or sensory tools like a glitter bottle. Keep it neutral and welcoming so the space signals comfort rather than punishment. When emotions run high, invite your child to use it. Once calm, have a short conversation about what happened and what to try differently next time.

A calm corner works because it offers recovery, not rejection. At home, it becomes a steady reminder that strong feelings can be managed in safe and supportive ways.

Strategy 10: Model The Behavior You Want To See

Children with ADHD pay closer attention to what you do than to what you say. Lectures often fade quickly, but your actions leave a strong impression. The clearest way to teach calm and self-control at home is to demonstrate them yourself.

Modeling behavior means practicing the same regulation you want your child to develop. When they see you pause before reacting, lower your voice instead of raising it, or breathe through a moment of tension, they learn by imitation.

One mother noticed her temper rising when her son spilled juice across the kitchen floor. Instead of snapping, she closed her eyes, took a slow breath, and then spoke in a steady voice: "Accidents happen, let's clean this together." Her son watched the pause more than he heard the words. Later that week, when he grew upset over a broken toy, he took a breath before asking for help. The technique had transferred without a lesson.

You can build the same influence in daily life. Slow your pace when you feel rushed, and your child will see that stress can be managed without shouting. State your feelings calmly instead of hiding them, so your child learns that strong emotions do not need to explode. Admit when you lose control and show how you return to balance, because mistakes are also part of the model.

Children develop self-control by watching it in action. At home, your steadiness becomes their guide, turning everyday discipline into a living example they can follow.

Chapter 4:
Strategies To Boost Emotional Strength And Self Esteem

"Children are not things to be molded, but people to be unfolded." —
Jess Lair

I t starts with a sentence that lands heavier than most parents realize.

At the dinner table, a boy fidgets in his chair, bouncing his leg and tapping a fork against the plate. His mother sighs and says, *"Why can't you sit still like your sister?"* The words aren't meant to wound. They're spoken out of fatigue after a long day. But the boy lowers his eyes. What he hears isn't about his behavior—it's about who he is. In his head, the message settles: *"Something is wrong with me."*

Children with ADHD hear more corrections than encouragement. They're told to try harder, calm down, listen, focus. Over time, the constant stream of what they are doing "wrong" shapes how they see themselves. Self-esteem drops. Frustration builds. Many begin to believe that no matter what they do, they'll never measure up. That belief is heavy, and it lingers.

Now picture the same moment handled differently. The boy is still restless, the tapping still loud. This time his mother leans closer and says, *"I see you have so much energy tonight. Let's use it to help me clear the table fast—I know you're quick."* His posture changes. He jumps up, races to gather plates, and beams when she adds, *"You're my best helper when it comes to speed."* Instead of shame, he feels capable. Instead of thinking he is the problem, he sees that his energy can be useful.

That shift—from criticism to encouragement—can transform a child's inner world. A single positive frame does not erase ADHD, nor does it end all struggles. But it plants a seed: *"I am more than my mistakes. I have strengths that matter."* When that seed is watered consistently, self-esteem grows and emotional strength takes root.

This chapter is here to help you create that growth. You'll find ten practical strategies designed to build resilience and a healthy self-image in your child. These aren't abstract ideas about confidence; they are daily actions you can take to help your child see themselves as strong, capable, and worthy.

You'll learn how to spot and celebrate your child's strengths, even when weaknesses feel louder. You'll see how simple changes in language—like turning *"You never listen"* into *"I love it when you pay attention, let's try again"*—reshape the way your child views themselves. You'll practice noticing small wins that are easy to overlook, and you'll discover how responsibility, problem-solving, friendships, traditions, and even stories of role models can become building blocks of self-worth.

Think of self-esteem as armor. Without it, every correction, every comparison, every failure cuts deep. With it, your child can handle challenges without losing their sense of value. Emotional strength doesn't mean they never stumble; it means they get back up believing they're still enough.

You don't need grand gestures to make this happen. What changes a child's view of themselves are the consistent, everyday interactions: the words you choose, the way you respond when they falter, the opportunities you give them to shine in small but meaningful ways.

In the pages ahead, you'll find ten strategies to help you do exactly that. Each one is simple enough to start today, yet powerful enough to shift how your child feels about who they are. With these tools, you can replace the echo of *"Why can't you...?"* with a steady chorus of

"You can." And that chorus, repeated over time, is what teaches your child to believe it.

Strategy 1: Focus On Strengths Not Only Weaknesses

Children with ADHD often hear more about what they can't do than what they can. "Why can't you sit still?" "You're always forgetting things." "Stop being so distracted." Even when meant as guidance, these comments pile up as constant reminders of shortcomings. Over time, your child begins to expect criticism, bracing for the next remark about what went wrong.

Focusing on strengths doesn't mean pretending difficulties don't exist. It means balancing the picture. Every child has qualities worth noticing—creativity, humor, imagination, determination, curiosity. When you highlight these, you give your child proof that they are more than their struggles.

Take Sophie, a seven-year-old who often left toys scattered across the living room. Her parents used to scold her: "You're so messy, why can't you clean up like other kids?" She would roll her eyes and drag her feet, convinced she was always failing. One day, her father shifted the focus. He noticed the detail she put into her Lego creations and said, "I love how creative you are with building. You think of designs I never would." Sophie lit up. The next time they asked her to clear the table, they framed it around her strength: "Use that same creative energy to see how fast you can arrange the plates." Instead of feeling criticized, she felt capable.

You can start this shift at home with small, specific feedback each day:

- Instead of "Good job," say: "You remembered to feed the dog without me asking—that shows responsibility."

- Instead of "You're smart," say: "I love how you figured out a new way to stack those blocks—that shows problem-solving."

This strategy is about daily family life, not school assignments or routines. Keep it focused on your child's personal qualities and the small ways they shine at home.

When you frame feedback this way, you give your child a mirror that reflects back their value, not just their mistakes. They begin to internalize the belief: *"I have qualities worth noticing."* Over time, that belief becomes the foundation of genuine self-esteem.

Seeing strengths first builds true self-esteem.

Strategy 2: Use Encouraging Language Every Day

The words you choose shape how your child sees themselves. For a child with ADHD, who already battles daily reminders of what is "too much" or "not enough," language becomes either a weight that pulls them down or a rope that lifts them up.

Think about the difference between these two phrases:

- *"You never listen."*

- *"I like it when you pay attention. Let's try again."*

The first shuts a door. It labels the child as someone who always fails. The second opens a door. It points out what you value and invites them to succeed. Both sentences are about the same behavior, but the impact could not be more different.

Children replay what they hear from you in their own minds. If most of your words highlight mistakes, they'll adopt that same harsh voice toward themselves. If they regularly hear encouragement, they carry that positivity into their self-talk. Over time, that difference shapes their confidence.

One mother, Carla, shared how her son would give up quickly when frustrated with a puzzle. Her instinct was to say, *"You're not even trying."* It only made him slam the pieces down harder. She shifted to: *"I see you're working hard. Let's try one more piece together."*

The change was immediate. Instead of storming off, he stayed and finished the puzzle. The words didn't just soften the moment—they helped him believe he could do it.

You don't need long speeches. In fact, short, specific praise works best:

- *"You waited your turn—that was respectful."*
- *"You kept trying even when it was tricky—that shows persistence."*
- *"I like how you explained your idea so clearly—that was thoughtful."*

When encouragement becomes part of your daily language, your child starts to expect affirmation, not just correction. They learn that their effort, kindness, and creativity are seen. And when they see themselves through that lens, self-esteem grows naturally.

Your words shape your child's self-image.

Strategy 3: Celebrate Small Wins Consistently

For children with ADHD, some of the most meaningful victories happen in small, ordinary moments at home. Picking up toys without being asked, finishing a short drawing, or letting a sibling go first may look minor, but each is a step worth noticing. When these efforts go unrecognized, children may feel unseen. When you highlight them, you show that everyday choices carry value.

Celebration does not require stickers or rewards. It works best through simple, immediate signals that say, "I noticed." A smile, a nod, or a high five can turn a small effort into pride. The impact lies in naming the behavior clearly so your child connects the recognition to what they just did.

Daniel, a father, struggled to keep his daughter engaged in activities. One afternoon she completed a beaded bracelet she normally abandoned halfway. Instead of offering a casual "good job," he knelt beside her and said, "You kept your focus until the end. That was real effort." She placed the bracelet in a box with a smile and asked to try again the next day. The acknowledgment fueled her persistence more than any reward could.

You can do the same in daily life:

- "You put your shoes by the door without me asking. That was responsible."

- "You stayed with the puzzle until the last piece. That was real concentration."

- "You shared your crayons with your brother. That was thoughtful."

These quick recognitions build confidence step by step. Over time, your child begins to connect effort with pride and sees themselves as capable of making good choices each day.

Small wins become the foundation for lasting self-belief when they are noticed right away.

Strategy 4: Encourage Independent Problem Solving

Children with ADHD often look for help the moment they hit a bump. At home this might mean asking you to fix a toy, reassemble a puzzle piece, or put crayons back in their box. If you always step in right away, your child learns to wait for rescue instead of learning that they can figure things out. Giving them space to try, even in small ways, builds the confidence that they can handle everyday challenges.

Imagine your child struggling with a toy box lid that won't close. Instead of fixing it yourself, you pause and ask, *"What do you think we should try first?"* They may push harder, turn it sideways, or even decide to take a few pieces out before trying again. The solution may not be perfect, but the act of trying shifts the focus from helplessness to capability.

One mother, Julia, saw this with her son during board games. Whenever a rule confused him, he would push the game aside in frustration. She began saying, *"Show me your idea, and let's see how it works."* Sometimes his solutions were unconventional, but they gave him ownership. Soon, he was less quick to give up and more willing to experiment.

These small scenarios happen every day:

- Puzzles: fitting the last piece without you guiding their hand.

- Crayons: figuring out how to slide them all back into a tight box.

- Toy cars: deciding their own way to line them up after play.

Each attempt strengthens the belief that they can solve problems without immediate help. Your role is not to supply the answer, but to create room for them to discover it.

At home, each small problem solved independently—whether it's a toy, a game, or a simple task—strengthens your child's confidence far more than being rescued.

Strategy 5: Create Opportunities For Responsibility At Home

For children with ADHD, responsibility at home is not about chores that feel like punishment. It's about small, everyday roles that give them a sense of being trusted and important. These moments help them build pride in themselves—not through schoolwork or rules, but through simple acts in family life.

Think of the difference between saying, *"Clean up this mess now,"* and, *"You're in charge of turning on the porch light every evening."* The first feels like an order; the second feels like a role. When a child knows a task is theirs to manage, they stand taller, even if it's something small.

Take Martin, an eight-year-old who often felt clumsy and "in the way." His parents gave him the job of turning on the porch light before dinner. It took only a few seconds, but he loved reminding the family if they forgot. Over time, he introduced himself proudly as "the light manager." That tiny task became a daily reminder that he could be counted on.

Here are examples of responsibilities that build confidence without overwhelming your child:

- Caring for something living: watering a plant, filling the pet's water bowl.

- Household helper roles: pressing the button to start the dishwasher, carrying mail inside, turning off the TV when it's bedtime.

- Keeping things in place: putting shoes neatly by the door each evening, placing napkins on the table before meals.

What matters is that these tasks are clear, consistent, and treated as your child's own role. If they spill water while feeding the dog or place the shoes slightly off-center, resist the urge to correct immediately. The goal is not perfection but ownership.

At home, even the smallest roles—like caring for a plant or turning on a light—help your child see themselves as capable and needed.

Strategy 6: Encourage Positive Peer Interactions

When play with others turns into interruptions, arguments, or impatience, your child may end up feeling left out. These moments can hurt more than they show. By guiding small, informal play opportunities at home or in the neighborhood, you can create interactions where they feel included and valued.

The focus here is not school settings or structured social skills. It's about simple, everyday moments—playdates with one or two friends, cousins visiting on the weekend, or a short game with a neighbor in the backyard—where you can shape the interaction into something positive.

Take Evan, a nine-year-old who often came home upset after neighborhood games ended in fights. His parents began inviting just one or two children over instead of large groups. They set up short, structured activities—like a Lego challenge or a baking project—that gave Evan clear ways to participate. With fewer kids and a defined game, he found it easier to stay engaged and enjoyed the feeling of belonging.

Another family saw success during cousin visits. Knowing that unstructured play often ended in conflict, they planned a simple treasure hunt in the backyard with clear rules and a time limit. The children laughed, cooperated, and finished together—leaving everyone with a memory of fun instead of tension.

You can support your child by:

- Keeping groups small: one or two peers create less pressure.
- Planning short activities: a 20-minute board game, baking cookies, or building a fort.
- Creating a clear beginning and end: this helps your child know what to expect and reduces stress.

These guided interactions don't need to happen every day. Even occasional, successful play experiences build a sense of competence in social situations.

At home and in small peer settings, even brief moments of successful play remind your child that friendship is possible and that they belong.

Strategy 7: Teach Your Child To Express Feelings With Words

When frustration builds, many children with ADHD turn to shouting, slamming, or storming off. These reactions come quickly because strong emotions feel overwhelming and words are hard to find in the moment. By giving your child simple ways to name their feelings, you help them pause and manage those emotions without letting them spill over into chaos.

This strategy is about family life—moments at home when your child is upset about a broken toy, a sibling argument, or a drawing that didn't come out the way they wanted. It's not about discipline or schoolwork, but about giving children the language to share emotions in safe, everyday contexts.

Take Mia, a six-year-old who often screamed when her block tower collapsed. Her parents introduced cards with simple faces—happy, sad, mad, worried. The next time the tower fell, instead of screaming, Mia pointed to the "mad" card and said, *"I feel mad."* That shift turned an outburst into an opening for comfort.

Another boy, Leo, used to yell when his sister borrowed his toys. His parents practiced a script: *"I feel upset when you take my car without asking."* At first he needed reminders, but with practice the words replaced the shouting.

Even in quieter moments, this practice helps. Emma once cried when her drawing got torn accidentally. With support, she managed to say, *"I feel sad my picture ripped."* Instead of spiraling into tears, she received empathy and was able to start again.

You can support your child with tools like:

- Emotion cards or charts: faces showing common feelings they can point to.

- A feelings notebook: a page with stickers or drawings for different moods.

- Modeling sentences: *"I feel frustrated when the TV remote doesn't work"* shows them how you use words yourself.

Every time your child says "I feel…" instead of acting out, they learn that emotions can be shared without fear and handled with words.

At home, giving children words for their feelings shows them that emotions can be shared and managed safely within the family.

Strategy 8: Create A Family Tradition To Celebrate Your Child

When much of the week feels full of reminders and corrections, a simple tradition that highlights your child's efforts can restore balance. These recurring moments create a predictable space where your child feels noticed and valued for who they are.

This strategy is about small, celebratory traditions within the family, not about chores, discipline, or collective bonding. The goal is to build something simple and personal that places your child in the spotlight for their genuine efforts.

One family created a Friday pizza night where their son always had the first turn to share a personal success from the week. Sometimes it was finishing a Lego design, sometimes it was showing kindness to a sibling. He looked forward to the evening, knowing that no matter how the week had gone, he would have a moment to be recognized.

Another parent started a "special choice night." Once a week, her daughter selected the family movie. The privilege was not tied to grades or chores but to the tradition itself, which quietly told her, "Your voice matters in this family."

You can adapt the idea in different ways:

- A weekly dinner where your child shares one thing they are proud of.

- A small "celebration board" where you post notes about personal wins.

- A rotating "choice night" where your child picks a meal, activity, or game.

What makes these traditions effective is their consistency. They do not need to be elaborate or festive. By repeating them week after week, you give your child steady proof that their contributions are seen and valued, even on difficult days.

A tradition that shines a light on individual effort helps your child carry a stronger sense of belonging and pride into the rest of family life.

Strategy 9: Encourage Physical Activities That Build Confidence

A child often discovers confidence through movement. The moment they reach the end of a swimming lane, land a karate kick with precision, or complete a dance routine, their body tells them what words alone cannot: "I can do this." Each physical milestone becomes proof of ability, building a sense of pride that stays long after the activity ends.

This strategy is not about daily exercise or burning off energy. Its purpose is to guide your child toward activities where progress is measured in small but meaningful achievements. Each new skill becomes a story they can carry with them, shaping a stronger view of themselves.

Noah, for example, often felt "behind" compared to peers. His parents signed him up for a beginner swim class. At first he splashed around aimlessly, but one evening he floated across the short side of the pool. The smile stayed on his face the whole evening, and the next week he asked to return with new determination. That single success reshaped how he saw himself.

You can offer the same opportunities with activities that emphasize progress rather than competition:

- Swimming lessons that celebrate each new stroke.

- Martial arts where respect and gradual skill-building are part of the journey.

- Dance classes where a short routine mastered step by step becomes a source of pride.

- Hiking or cycling routes where completing the path feels like a shared victory.

Each of these experiences offers your child a concrete marker of success. The pride gained in one activity often spills into other areas of life, strengthening self-belief and resilience.

Confidence grows when children experience achievement with their own bodies. These small wins remind them that they are capable and that their effort matters.

Strategy 10: Share Stories Of Role Models With ADHD

Stories can be powerful mirrors. When children hear about others who face the same challenges and still succeed, they begin to see new possibilities for themselves. These stories don't belong in classrooms or formal lessons—they work best at home, woven naturally into family conversations during dinner, car rides, or bedtime.

The point is not to list famous names but to make ADHD feel less isolating and more like a part of a larger story. Role models should feel accessible and relatable, so your child can think, *"That could be me."*

One father told his son about a neighbor who also had ADHD and used his endless energy to become a skilled carpenter. The boy, who often got teased for being restless, was fascinated by the idea that someone with the same challenges could build beautiful furniture with steady hands.

Another family shared the story of a musician with ADHD who turned constant tapping into rhythm and songwriting. Their daughter, who was always drumming on the table, suddenly saw her habit not as a flaw but as a sign of creativity.

You can choose from different kinds of role models:

- Athletes or artists who show how energy and creativity can be channeled into achievement.

- Friends, relatives, or neighbors who live with ADHD and have built meaningful lives.

- Inventors or entrepreneurs who explain that curiosity and persistence shaped their success.

What matters most is the message: others with ADHD have faced challenges, found their path, and created lives they are proud of.

At home, these stories help children see ADHD not as a barrier but as part of their identity, one that can fuel strengths and future success.

Chapter 5:
Strategies To Help Children Develop Social Skills

"Social skills are the tools children use to turn strangers into friends." — Michele Borba

Y ou're at the park, watching your child jump into a game of tag. He runs fast, shouts the rules over everyone, and tags before the countdown even starts. Two kids step back. One whispers, "He cheats." Minutes later, he's circling the group with his shoulders tight, insisting he didn't do anything wrong. You call him over; he's frustrated and confused. He wanted to play. He just didn't know how to fit.

Scenes like this can chip away at a child's social life. Interrupting, grabbing, and missing cues don't look like small slips to other kids; they feel unfair. Over time, that mismatch turns into fewer invitations and more "not today." Your child isn't broken or unkind. The issue is skill—not character. Social moves that come naturally to others need to be taught and practiced the same way you'd teach tying shoes.

Now picture the same park a few weeks later. Before joining, your child asks, "Can I play?" He waits through one round because that's the agreed start. When he gets excited, he squeezes a stress ball you tucked in his pocket instead of shouting over the group. A boy on the bench waves him in for the next turn. Your child finishes the game smiling, sweaty, and—most important—included. Nothing magical happened. You coached a few specific behaviors, practiced at home for short bursts, and set him up to try them in a low-pressure way.

That's the work of this chapter. You'll focus on practical, bite-size skills that help your child enter play, stay in play, and repair small bumps without drama. No lectures about "being nicer." No complicated systems. Just clear moves you can teach and rehearse in minutes, then bring into real life when the moment shows up.

You'll start with the foundation: waiting and taking turns so games feel fair to everyone. You'll add tools that make conversations smoother—how to listen without interrupting, how to start talking without freezing, and how to stay on the topic that's actually on the table. You'll help your child read faces and bodies so they notice when someone's bored, annoyed, or excited. You'll plan short, structured playdates that give peers a good first experience together. And because mistakes will happen, you'll teach simple repair language— quick apologies that reopen the door instead of closing it. Across these pages you'll find ten concrete strategies designed only for social skills with peers, not self-esteem work, discipline rules, routines, or school plans.

Here's how a tough moment can turn. During a block-building game, your child snatches a piece and a friend yells, "Hey!" In the past, that spark might have ended the playdate. After practice, your child says, "I'm sorry I grabbed your block. You can use mine, and I'll wait." The friend shrugs, hands a block back, and the tower continues. It's not perfect harmony; it's a repair that keeps the game alive.

As you move through this chapter, think small and specific. Choose one skill, practice it for a week in short, playful reps, and take it to the playground or a cousin visit. Notice what worked, tweak what didn't, and keep going. Social confidence grows one fair turn, one calm "Can I play?", one quick repair at a time. By the end, you'll have a set of tools your child can carry into any backyard, birthday party, or park— and use to turn almost-friends into real ones.

Strategy 1: Teach Turn Taking With Simple Games

At home or in a small group of friends, waiting for a turn can feel almost impossible. Impulsivity makes it tempting to jump in before others are ready, and what should be a shared game quickly turns into frustration for everyone. Other children may see this as unfair, and the risk is that play ends early or invitations stop coming.

Short games with clear rules create the right practice ground. Unlike open-ended play, board and card games provide a natural sequence where each person must wait. The rule is simple and visible: one player acts, then the next. This turns the vague instruction "be patient" into something concrete your child can practice and repeat.

Keep it brief. Games like Memory, Uno, or Connect Four are perfect because each round is fast and gives multiple chances to practice waiting. Long or complex activities often lead to restlessness and defeat the purpose. Ten minutes at a time is enough to build the skill without overwhelming your child.

One father noticed that his daughter would often grab puzzle pieces before others had placed theirs. To practice, they started playing short rounds of Connect Four together. At first, she tried to drop her piece before his turn, but he calmly reminded her of the rule and praised every moment she waited. After a week, she was proudly saying, "Your turn!" before making her move. When her cousin came over, she carried this habit into their play, and the game finished with laughter instead of arguments.

To make this work:

- Choose only short, structured games.
- Limit sessions to about 10–15 minutes.
- Sit close enough to give reminders if needed.
- Highlight success right away: "You waited—that made the game more fun."

Turn taking isn't just about games. Each time your child learns to pause and let others go first, they build trust with peers and gain confidence in their ability to join play without conflict. That sense of "I can do this" is what helps them feel welcome in future interactions.

Strategy 2: Practice Active Listening Through Role Play

During playdates or family conversations, children often get so eager to speak that they cut others off mid-sentence. What feels like enthusiasm to them can come across as dismissive or rude to others. Over time, this habit can make it harder to form or maintain friendships.

Role play offers a playful way to practice the skill of listening before speaking. By turning it into a short exercise, you help your child learn how to pause, echo what they've heard, and then add their own thought.

Keep the activity light and brief. Sit together and trade short sentences or mini-stories. After one person speaks, the listener repeats the last idea before responding. This slows down the impulse to interrupt and makes listening an active part of the exchange.

For example, one parent pretended to tell a funny story about the family dog knocking over a glass of water. The child's job was to echo a piece of the story—"The dog knocked over the water"—before reacting with their own comment. At first he jumped in too quickly, but with reminders he began to enjoy the rhythm of waiting, repeating, and then adding his words. Later, when chatting with a friend, he surprised his parent by nodding and echoing before giving his opinion, which kept the conversation going smoothly.

You can make it work by:

- Keeping sessions short, five to ten minutes at most.
- Using familiar topics—what happened at school, a favorite show, or a recent outing.

- Praising the effort as soon as it happens: "You waited and repeated what I said—that showed you were really listening."

When your child practices active listening at home and with peers, others begin to see them as respectful and enjoyable company, which strengthens friendships.

Strategy 3: Teach How To Recognize Facial Expressions And Body Language

In everyday play with siblings or friends, much of the communication happens without words. A frown, a smile, or folded arms can change the mood of the game. Some children don't notice these signals, and that can lead to arguments or misunderstandings—like continuing a joke when someone else is already annoyed.

This strategy is about practicing those cues in short, playful ways at home or with familiar peers. The goal is not therapy or formal lessons, but quick games that make noticing emotions part of ordinary social life.

One parent used picture cards of faces showing different feelings. At the kitchen table, they held one up and asked, "Which face looks worried?" Their child pointed and guessed, turning it into a fun round of "feelings bingo." Another evening, the family acted out body language instead—slumping shoulders for sadness, bouncing feet for excitement—and took turns guessing. These few minutes of practice, done casually, made it easier for their son to pick up on cues during playdates.

The Lego game is another good example. A boy who often grabbed pieces without noticing how others felt began to recognize frustration when his cousin frowned at the tower. After practicing at home, he stopped, looked, and asked, "Do you want me to wait?" The tower grew taller, and the play kept going without a fight.

You can make this work by:

- Using flashcards or printed faces for a quick guessing game.

- Acting out emotions as a family for a few minutes after dinner.

- Keeping sessions short and light—five minutes is enough.

- Praising every correct guess: "Yes, that looked like happy—you noticed it right away."

Recognizing expressions helps children adjust their behavior during play, keeping games going and friendships stronger.

Strategy 4: Create Short and Structured Playdates

Playdates work best when they are short, simple, and predictable. In informal settings at home or with just one or two peers, children have the chance to enjoy each other's company without the overwhelm that comes from large groups or unstructured hours of play.

The key is to choose activities that are easy to manage and naturally include everyone. Sixty to ninety minutes is usually enough—long enough to share an experience, but short enough to prevent fatigue or conflict.

One family invited a neighbor over for a pizza-making afternoon. Each child had their own small piece of dough and a few toppings to choose from. The activity was fun, brief, and had a clear beginning and end, which made it easy for the children to stay engaged.

Another parent set up a Lego challenge: each child had ten minutes to add their piece to a shared design. The short time frame and clear rules kept everyone focused and reduced arguments. A similar idea worked with cupcake decorating, where each child had two cupcakes and a small set of decorations—simple, quick, and satisfying.

To keep playdates successful:

- Limit the group to one or two peers.

- Plan activities that last no more than 15–20 minutes each.

- Guide gently if needed, but let the children lead the pace.

- End while energy is still positive, rather than stretching it until arguments begin.

Each short, structured playdate adds to your child's experience of friendship, showing them that social time can feel safe, predictable, and enjoyable.

Strategy 5: Teach How To Apologize and Repair After Mistakes

In social play at home or with a small group of peers, conflicts happen easily. A toy gets snatched, a block tower is knocked down, or a loud word slips out in the heat of the moment. Without guidance, these situations can end the game and leave children reluctant to play together again.

Practicing short, clear ways to apologize helps children understand that mistakes don't have to end friendships. Simple scripts make the process less intimidating and easier to remember. A phrase like, *"I'm sorry I grabbed your toy. Let's play together,"* both admits the mistake and reopens the door to play.

One parent used this approach when her son knocked over his cousin's block tower. Instead of letting the day end in frustration, she guided him to say, "I'm sorry I knocked it down. Can I help rebuild it?" The cousin agreed, and soon they were laughing as they rebuilt the tower side by side.

Another common scenario happened during drawing time. Two siblings fought over the same box of crayons. Their father stepped in, handed each child a few crayons, and prompted his son to say, "Sorry I took them all. You can use these, and I'll use these." The small repair allowed the activity to continue instead of breaking down in conflict.

To build this skill:

- Keep apology scripts short and concrete.

- Practice with role play at home—taking turns with a favorite toy car, bumping into each other, or sharing art supplies.

- Step in quickly during play to guide an apology before feelings harden.

- Praise the effort: "You said sorry right away—that helped your friend feel better."

Each time your child apologizes and repairs, they learn that friendships are not fragile—they can bend, adjust, and grow stronger.

Strategy 6: Encourage Sharing Through Guided Activities

In moments of play at home or during very small playdates, sharing often feels tricky. A child may clutch a toy, a crayon, or a snack, afraid that giving it up means they won't get it back. Left unchecked, these moments can lead to frustration and arguments.

Guided activities create a safe, playful way to practice sharing. The idea is not to lecture or demand, but to build short tasks where sharing is naturally part of the process. This turns "giving up" into an enjoyable step in the game.

Cooking together is a simple example. One child stirs the bowl, then passes the spoon to a sibling to add an ingredient. Everyone gets a role, and the turns move quickly. Puzzles work the same way: each child places one piece, then passes the next to a partner. Because the rules are clear and the activity is short, sharing feels easy instead of forced.

Other everyday scenarios can be just as effective. A parent can guide siblings to take turns watering a plant, passing the cup carefully back and forth. Or during play with an electronic toy, one child presses the button to make the lights flash, then hands it to the next for their turn. These quick exchanges show that sharing doesn't stop the fun—it keeps it going.

To make this work:

- Choose short, easy activities where sharing is built into the steps.

- Keep the group small, ideally siblings or one or two friends.

- Use simple prompts: "Now it's your turn, then your friend's turn."

- Offer immediate praise: "You passed the cup—that made the game fun for both of you."

At home, these small guided activities show children that sharing is not losing—it's what makes play with others possible and fun.

Strategy 7: Teach Simple Conversation Starters

In small playdates or informal family interactions, the hardest part is often taking the first step. A child may want to join in but stays silent, or blurts out something unrelated, making it harder for others to respond. These moments can leave them on the edge of the game instead of feeling part of it.

Conversation starters give children a simple way in. Short, ready-made phrases act like small bridges that connect them to others without pressure to invent words on the spot.

Keep the phrases few and practical, such as:

- "Can I play?"

- "What's your favorite game?"

- "Can I help with the puzzle?"

One mother practiced this with her son before a playdate. Together they rehearsed saying, "Can I play?" when other children were building with blocks. At first he was nervous, but once he tried it, the children welcomed him and made room in the game. Another parent encouraged a sibling to use a starter at home—"Can I help with the puzzle?"—during family play. The practice in a safe setting made it easier to use the same words later with friends.

To build confidence with starters:

- Practice at home through short role plays.

- Limit the list to two or three phrases at a time.

- Praise every attempt: "You asked politely—that helped you join in."

With just a few practiced starters, children learn that they can enter play smoothly, which makes peers more likely to welcome them again.

Strategy 8: Practice Staying On Topic During Talks

In informal family conversations or short playdates, it's common for children to jump quickly from one subject to another. A peer might be talking about soccer, and suddenly the topic shifts to video games or a random story. What feels natural to your child can leave others confused or less interested in continuing the exchange.

You can guide this skill by practicing "staying with the topic" in playful, short exercises at home. The aim is not to restrict imagination but to give your child the social tool to connect more smoothly with others in everyday interactions.

One parent noticed that her son often interrupted his cousin's story about school with sudden comments about cartoons. To practice, she set a simple dinner-table game: every answer had to include at least one word from the topic being discussed. If the topic was soccer, the child could say, "I kicked the ball today," before adding anything else. This small change made it easier for him to stay connected when chatting with peers.

Another family created a game of "topic tag." One sibling started with a sentence about pets, and the others had to respond with something linked—"My dog barks a lot," or "Cats like to sleep"—before moving to a new subject. The game was short, light, and showed how conversations flow better when ideas stay linked for a while.

To make practice work:

- Keep sessions short, just a few minutes.

- Choose everyday topics children enjoy—pets, favorite foods, recent games.

- Give immediate praise: "You stayed on soccer—that made it easy for us to keep talking."

When children practice staying on topic in small, familiar settings, they see that conversations become easier to follow. This helps peers enjoy talking with them and makes it more likely they'll be included again.

Strategy 9: Teach How To Handle Rejection Calmly

In small playdates at home or during informal family play with siblings or cousins, rejection is bound to happen. A child may hear, "No, I don't want to play that," or "Not right now." For some, these words feel like a door slamming shut, and the reaction can be anger, tears, or walking away in frustration.

You can prepare your child by practicing short, calm responses in advance. The goal isn't to deliver long explanations or polite speeches, but to give them a few realistic, child-sized phrases they can use to move past the moment.

One parent noticed her daughter would shout whenever her cousin refused to play dolls. Together they practiced saying, "That's okay, I'll play with something else." At the next playdate, when the cousin said no, she took a breath, used the phrase, and picked up a puzzle instead. Later, the cousin joined in, and the play continued peacefully.

Another family used toy cars for practice. One sibling said, "No, not this car right now," and the child's job was to reply calmly: "Okay, I'll wait for another turn." At first it felt forced, but after a few rounds, the child started using the same response naturally during play.

To build this habit:

- Keep the role-plays short and light.

- Stick to simple phrases like, "That's okay, I'll try something else," or "I'll wait."

- Praise calm reactions: "You stayed cool when I said no—that made it easier to keep playing."

At home and in small peer play, learning to handle "no" calmly shows children that rejection doesn't end the fun—it keeps the door open for more play together.

Strategy 10: Model Positive Social Behavior At Home

Children learn how to interact by watching the people around them. Simple gestures of politeness at home, such as saying thank you, waiting for a turn, or passing an object with care, become the patterns they repeat with siblings, cousins, and friends.

The most effective way to teach these habits is not through lectures but through consistent example. When you show respect in small everyday actions, your child sees how courtesy works in practice and begins to copy it.

One mother thanked her son each time he handed her a spoon while cooking. Before long, he began using the same words with his sister during play: "Thanks for giving me the block." Another parent, while playing a board game, said aloud, "Your turn," as he let his daughter go first. She later repeated the same courtesy with a classmate. Even at the dinner table, a simple "thank you" when someone passes the salt sends a signal that children quickly absorb.

To make this part of daily life:

- Use short phrases of gratitude that are easy to repeat.

- Show patience in small interactions, such as waiting calmly in line or letting someone speak before you.

- Practice the same gestures with both adults and children so your child sees that respect applies everywhere.

What children witness at home becomes the foundation of how they behave with others. When kindness and courtesy are modeled consistently, social interactions feel smoother and friendships have stronger ground to grow.

One Minute That Matters

Sometimes the smallest gestures carry the most weight. A short review may not seem like much, but for another parent it can be the moment they feel less alone or finally see that change is possible.

When someone is deciding whether to pick up this book, they often look at reviews first. Your honest thoughts can guide them. You don't have to write anything long or polished. A few sentences about what was helpful, what gave you a new idea, or even what you struggled with can make a real difference.

I read every review personally and I am grateful for all of them, positive or negative. Honest feedback is what helps this work grow and reach the families who need it most.

If these pages have given you even a little encouragement, please consider sharing your experience. That single act can carry hope from your home to someone else's.

Scan to leave a review on Amazon

Chapter 6: Strategies To Strengthen Communication And Connection

"To connect with your child, you must listen with your heart more than with your ears." — Gordon Neufeld

You're chopping vegetables in the kitchen when your child wanders in.

"How was your day?" you ask.

"Fine."

"Anything fun happen?"

"Nothing."

Each word feels like a wall. You want to hear more, but the conversation shrinks until it disappears. By the time you set dinner on the table, you're carrying a quiet ache: the sense that your child's world is just out of reach.

Moments like this happen often with ADHD. Communication can become clipped, defensive, or scattered, leaving both of you frustrated. Over time, unanswered questions and short replies create a distance that neither side intends, but both can feel.

Now imagine the same scene with a small shift. Instead of rushing to fill the silence, you pause, notice the way his shoulders slump, and say, "Looks like today wore you out." His head lifts. "Yeah... recess was rough." You lean on the counter, giving him space. "Want to tell me about it?" Slowly, the words come. A story unfolds, and in those few minutes, you've built a bridge instead of letting silence stand between you.

That contrast—between a conversation that closes down and one that opens up—is the heart of this chapter. Communication with a child who has ADHD is not only about exchanging words; it's about building connection in the everyday moments when your child decides whether to let you in or shut you out.

Think of a common "before and after" exchange:

Before

Parent: "Why didn't you clean your room like I asked?"

Child: "I don't know. Stop bothering me!"

Parent: "You never listen. Go do it now."

Child: "You're so mean!"

After

Parent: "I saw you started cleaning and then got distracted. Want me to help with the first part?"

Child: "Okay."

Parent: "Great. Once we do the clothes, you can try the rest."

Child: "Yeah, I can do that."

The task hasn't changed, but the tone has. One path leads to conflict; the other builds cooperation.

This chapter will guide you through ten practical strategies designed to make those "after" conversations happen more often. They're not about discipline, schoolwork, or peer interactions. They're about the bond between you and your child—the daily words, tones, and gestures that decide whether family life feels like a series of clashes or a place of safety and understanding.

When communication flows, trust deepens. When trust deepens, connection grows. And when connection grows, even the hardest days become easier to face together.

Strategy 1: Use Eye Level Conversations To Improve Attention

When you call instructions from across the room, your words compete with every sound, thought, and distraction already swirling in your child's mind. To you, it feels like being ignored. To your child, it feels like background noise.

A small physical shift changes that: move closer, lower yourself to their level, and wait until their eyes meet yours. In that moment, your child knows you are speaking *with* them, not *at* them. The difference is not just practical—it is relational. It tells them, "I see you, and you matter enough for me to stop what I'm doing and meet you here."

Picture this scene: your son is sprawled on the carpet, building a tower. You kneel beside him and say quietly, "Look at me for a second." His eyes lift. "Dinner's ready—let's wash hands." The tower is still tempting, but the words land because they were carried by connection, not distance.

The goal isn't to shorten commands—that belongs elsewhere. Here, the goal is to create a channel of attention where listening can happen. Children with ADHD are far more likely to tune in when they feel included and respected, not shouted at from another room.

This approach also reduces tension. Instead of a power struggle— "You never listen!" "Stop yelling at me!"—it becomes an invitation into shared space. The act of bending down, pausing, and seeking eye contact is a gesture of respect. It softens the exchange and opens a window for cooperation.

You don't need long speeches or forced eye contact that makes your child uncomfortable. Just a brief glance, a short phrase, and a physical presence beside them. These moments of alignment cut through distraction and build trust over time.

Connection starts with seeing eye to eye.

Strategy 2: Use Clear And Simple Language

Sometimes your child seems to shut down not because they don't want to listen, but because your words come in a long stream that feels impossible to follow. By the time you've finished explaining, their attention has already drifted somewhere else. What you meant as guidance lands instead as noise.

Simpler language changes that. When you use short, concrete phrases, your child has a better chance of holding the meaning in their mind and acting on it. It's not about giving orders; it's about removing the clutter so communication feels doable.

Imagine a parent calling from the kitchen: "In a few minutes it's time to stop playing, put your toys away, wash your hands, and come sit down because dinner will be ready." By the time the sentence is over, the child is restless, confused, or already tuned out. Compare that with walking over and saying warmly, "Dinner time—wash hands first." The message is brief, but it carries the same care, and now the child knows exactly what to do next.

These small adjustments reduce stress on both sides. Your child doesn't feel overwhelmed by too much information, and you don't have to repeat yourself ten times. Over time, this creates an atmosphere where communication feels less like nagging and more like support.

You can make this part of daily life by choosing just a few words at a time. Break bigger requests into smaller pieces: "Homework out." Pause. Then, "Pencil ready." Each step becomes manageable, and your child experiences the success of completing it. That success feeds motivation and keeps the interaction positive.

The heart of this strategy is accessibility. Simple words help your child understand what you mean without feeling pressured or lost. And when understanding is easier, cooperation comes more naturally.

Short words carry farther.

Strategy 3: Practice Reflective Listening To Show Understanding

Children with ADHD often feel that adults don't really "get" them. When they explode or complain, what they hear in return is often correction, minimization, or advice. That response can leave them feeling more alone in their frustration.

Reflective listening is a way for you, as the parent, to show that you are tuned in. It's not about teaching your child new words—that belongs elsewhere. It's about mirroring back the essence of what they've said so they know you are with them emotionally.

One evening your daughter slams her backpack on the floor and blurts out, "I hate school!" The instinct to reply, "Don't talk like that" is strong, but it shuts the moment down. Instead, you take a breath and say, "You sound really frustrated with school today." She pauses, her voice softens: "Yeah... my teacher moved my seat and I couldn't focus." The anger starts to melt, and now the conversation has space to grow.

To practice reflective listening, keep it short and centered on the feeling behind the words:

- "You felt left out when that happened."
- "You're upset because the game ended too soon."
- "You sound disappointed that it didn't turn out how you hoped."

This doesn't mean letting everything slide. You can still set boundaries: "I hear how angry you are. I won't allow hurtful words, but I want to understand what's underneath." Reflection opens the door; the limit keeps the structure.

When your child feels heard, listening back to you becomes much easier.

Strategy 4: Use Family Check In Moments Daily

Not every conversation has to be long or carefully planned. Sometimes the most powerful connections come from a two-minute pause, where your child feels you've noticed them and want to hear a fragment of their day. For a child with ADHD, those micro-windows matter—they're short enough to hold attention, but steady enough to build trust.

These check-ins aren't family rituals or weekly traditions. They don't require pizza nights or long talks on the couch. They're quick touchpoints that can fit anywhere: the car ride to practice, the first minutes of dinner, or a pause before lights out.

One parent found that asking, "What made you smile today?" worked best in the car. Her son rarely opened up at bedtime, but the moment his seatbelt clicked, he was ready to talk. The setting didn't matter—the consistency of a daily check-in did.

You can keep it light with simple prompts like:

- "What was the best part of your day?"
- "Was there something that felt tricky?"

These aren't interviews. They're invitations. Over time, your child learns that each day holds a space where their voice counts, no matter how big or small the story is.

Connection grows in small daily doses.

Strategy 5: Use Visual Aids To Support Communication

For a child with ADHD, spoken words can slip away quickly. Explanations may blur together, especially when emotions are high. In those moments, adding something visual gives the message weight—it makes the abstract more concrete.

These visual aids are not charts for routines or checklists for schoolwork. They're quick, improvised cues you use in the middle of a conversation: a doodle on scrap paper, a symbol with your hands, a simple card pulled from a drawer. They work because they anchor words in something your child can see.

One parent, faced with constant arguments about choices, began sketching options instead of repeating them. When her son resisted deciding between outdoor play and reading, she drew a ball on one side of the page and a book on the other. "Which one feels right for now?" she asked. Seeing the choice made it less overwhelming, and he pointed without another fight.

Another family used simple drawings to talk about emotions. When their daughter was too upset to explain herself, her father grabbed a sticky note and quickly drew a sun, a cloud, and a lightning bolt. "Which one is closest to how you feel?" She tapped the lightning bolt. From there, he could say, "That storm inside feels strong—I'm here with you." The picture opened a door words alone could not.

These moments don't require artistic skill or special materials. A pen, a scrap of paper, or a small set of picture cards are enough. What matters is the immediacy: you translate feelings or choices into images that your child can grasp in real time.

Pictures make words easier to hold.

Strategy 6: Use Storytelling To Teach And Connect

Children remember stories long after they forget lectures. For a child with ADHD—who may tune out when conversations sound like lessons—stories bring meaning in a form that feels alive.

This isn't about heroes or role models—that belongs elsewhere. Here it's about your own small, imperfect stories. Moments when you messed up, laughed at yourself, or had to fix a mistake. These simple memories show your child that everyone stumbles and that mistakes don't erase connection.

One father used this when his son forgot his shoes for the third time. Instead of scolding, he said, "When I was your age, I once walked halfway to school in slippers before I noticed. I had to run back, embarrassed and laughing at myself." His son burst out laughing, and the tension eased. Then the father added, "Everyone forgets sometimes. Let's figure out a way to remember tomorrow." The lesson landed because it was wrapped in a story, not a lecture.

Another parent, when her daughter felt guilty about yelling at her brother, briefly shared how she had snapped at her own sister as a child and then made up later. The girl looked surprised: "So you did that too?" That moment of recognition softened her shame.

Stories don't need to be dramatic. They work best when they're short, honest, and tied to the moment at hand. Try sharing one small story tonight and see how your child reacts—you may find they remember it long after your advice would have faded.

Strategy 7: Use Physical Affection As A Communication Tool

Not every message needs words. Sometimes what reaches your child most clearly is a gesture—a squeeze of the hand, an arm around the shoulder, a playful high five. For children with ADHD, who may hear constant reminders or corrections during the day, these moments of physical affection cut through the noise and deliver a simple message: *you are loved, right now, as you are.*

Affection doesn't replace language; it prepares the ground for it. A light touch when your child is upset can make them more open to listening a few minutes later. A hug before school can turn into the confidence to face the day. A quiet pat on the back after effort can soften the space for words of encouragement.

What works best depends on your child's age and temperament. A younger child might sink into a big embrace, while a preteen may prefer a quick fist bump or sitting shoulder to shoulder without saying much. Adapting the gesture keeps it genuine and respectful.

Used consistently, these small acts create an invisible net of safety. They remind your child that closeness is always available, not just when things go well. And often, the memory of a touch lingers even longer than the words spoken alongside it.

For many children, that quiet squeeze of the hand will be remembered long after the words are forgotten.

Strategy 8: Teach Your Child To Use "I Statements"

When emotions run high, it's easy for a child with ADHD to lash out with blame: "You're mean!" "You always take my stuff!" These words come quickly, but they push others away and often make conflicts worse. What your child may not know is that there's another way to say the same thing—one that lets their feelings be heard without turning into a fight.

That's where "I statements" come in. Teaching your child to start with "I feel..." helps them describe their own experience instead of attacking the other person. The difference seems small, but it changes the whole tone of the exchange.

For example:

- Instead of: "You never let me play!"
- Try: "I feel sad when I don't get a turn."
- Instead of: "You're so mean!"
- Try: "I feel hurt when my toy is taken."

At first, you may need to model it yourself. One mother noticed her son yelling, "You're unfair!" when his brother grabbed a game controller. She stepped in and said, "I feel frustrated when I'm left out of the game. Can we try again?" Then she gently asked her son to try the same structure: "I feel upset when you take it without asking." With practice, the angry accusations began turning into clearer statements of need.

This strategy is not about teaching your child a script to recite mechanically. It's about giving them a tool to express emotions in a way that invites understanding. Over time, "I statements" reduce the blame in family conversations and help siblings, parents, and the child themselves hear the real feeling underneath the outburst.

You can encourage this skill by pausing in the moment and offering gentle prompts: "Try starting with 'I feel…' instead of 'You always…'." Keep it light, and praise the effort even if the sentence isn't perfect. The goal is practice, not perfection.

When blame turns into ownership of feelings, connection becomes easier, and problems get solved faster.

Strategy 9: Create Rituals Of Connection

At the doorway before school, a boy waits for his father's hand. They slap palms twice, then lock thumbs in a secret shake that lasts only a moment. It is playful, fast, and ordinary, yet it steadies him as he climbs onto the bus. Small gestures like this work as anchors, showing a child that closeness with a parent is always there.

These rituals are not big family traditions or celebrations. They are brief exchanges shared only between you and your child, built to be quick, repeatable, and personal.

One mother sang the same short tune each night as she tucked in her daughter. The melody was simple, but it became a signal that the day was closing with comfort and safety. Another parent whispered a silly phrase at bedtime that always brought a smile. Over time, these moments grew into markers of stability, independent of how the rest of the day had gone.

You can invent similar rituals with ease:

- A special clap before saying goodnight.

- A phrase spoken in the car before drop-off.

- A light tap on the shoulder followed by a smile at the same moment each evening.

The power of these rituals lies in their predictability. They tell your child that no matter how chaotic the day has been, this shared signal will remain. With repetition, these small acts give lasting reassurance that your bond is steady and secure.

Strategy 10: End The Day With Positive Words

The last moments before sleep carry a special weight. For a child with ADHD—whose day may have been filled with corrections, frustrations, and reminders—what you say as they drift off can shape how they remember the whole day.

This isn't about bedtime routines like pajamas or brushing teeth—that belongs elsewhere. It isn't about gestures or songs either—that's another kind of ritual. Here the focus is on words: the final sentences your child hears before sleep.

Those words should not be a review of the day or a lesson about tomorrow. They are not the time for reminders or corrections. They are a chance to leave your child with comfort, belonging, and the certainty that they are loved.

One mother chose to whisper every night, "I'm proud of how hard you tried today." Even on evenings marked by tears over homework, her son went to sleep knowing his effort mattered. Another parent simply said, "I love you no matter what." Her daughter began repeating the phrase back before closing her eyes, holding it like a shield against the day's worries.

Your bedtime words might be as simple as:

- "I liked how you kept going, even when it was tough."

- "I love being your mom/dad."

- "Tomorrow is a new day, and I'll be here with you."

Over time, this consistent closing message becomes part of the emotional rhythm of your child's nights. They may not remember the exact words, but they carry the feeling: the day always ends with reassurance.

The last words of the day often stay with children long after the light is turned off.

Chapter 7:
Strategies To Improve Sleep, Nutrition, And Physical Activity

"A child's body is the engine of learning. When sleep, food, and movement are balanced, the mind runs smoothly." — Anonymous

B edtime turns into negotiations. "Two more pages... one more video... I'm not tired." Lights go out late, and morning starts with a heavy head and a quiet "I'm not hungry." By mid-day your child is parked in a chair, fingers twitching while the rest of the body barely moves. The day feels sticky. Small frustrations pop faster. Focus slips, patience thins, and by evening their eyes are wide again just when you want them to slow down.

That pattern isn't about willpower. It's a body running on uneven inputs. Too little sleep makes thinking feel foggy and emotions jagged. Skipped or sugary meals spike energy and then drop it hard. Hours without movement leave the nervous system revved with nowhere to go. When those three pieces—sleep, food, movement—fall out of rhythm, ADHD symptoms get louder. You see more fidgeting, more irritability, more "I can't."

Now picture a different day. Bedtime lands at a clear hour. The room is dim and quiet, and screens are off well before lights out. Morning starts with a small, steady breakfast—yogurt with fruit or eggs and toast—and a glass of water. Sometime after school there's real movement: a bike ride around the block, a game of tag, a fast walk with the dog. That night your child falls asleep faster and stays asleep longer. The next afternoon, they still have gas in the tank instead of crashing on the couch.

One family made two changes in one week: screens off an hour before bed and a protein-forward breakfast. Their son used to melt down around 11:30 a.m. and needed constant snacks by 3:00 p.m. After a few days, the late-morning crash eased. He was less snappy in the afternoon, and bedtime stopped dragging past ten. Nothing else changed—same school, same homework, same house. Different inputs, different day.

This chapter gives you ten practical moves to tune those inputs. You'll set a consistent sleep window that holds even on weekends. You'll build a wind-down that actually calms a busy brain. You'll cut evening screens so the body's "sleep switch" flips on time. You'll use regular meals and simple swaps—more protein, fewer sugary drinks—to keep energy steady. You'll add daily movement that fits real life, not a perfect schedule.

You won't be asked to overhaul your household. Pick one strategy. Try it for a week. Watch what shifts: fewer morning standoffs, fewer afternoon dips, fewer bedtime battles. Then stack a second strategy on top of the first. Small, boring consistency beats big, heroic efforts that last two days.

Here's the lens to keep: your child's brain rides on their body. When sleep is predictable, food is steady, and movement is daily, the rest of the day runs smoother. Focus stretches a bit longer. Frustrations pass a bit faster. Evenings soften. That relief isn't magic—it's physiology working for you instead of against you.

Ready? Start with the piece that will give you the quickest win in your home—bedtime, breakfast, or movement—and build from there. Each of the ten strategies that follow is simple, concrete, and designed for families who are already tired. The goal is a body that supports a brain with ADHD, so your child can bring more of their best self to the day.

Strategy 1: Set A Consistent Bedtime And Wake Up Time

This strategy is about when your child goes to bed and wakes up—not about what they do to get ready for sleep, not about bedtime rituals, and not about the emotional tone of the evening. The focus here is simply on keeping a steady clock.

Children with ADHD often resist bedtime with endless requests— "five more minutes," "just one more show"—and then struggle to wake the next morning. The constant shift between late nights and chaotic mornings leaves them groggy, irritable, and less able to focus during the day.

A consistent sleep schedule creates stability. When your child goes to bed and wakes up at the same times every day, including weekends, their body learns what to expect. Instead of fighting sleep, their system gradually aligns with a rhythm. Over time, it becomes easier to fall asleep at night and to get up without a battle in the morning.

One family decided that 9:00 p.m. would always be lights-out, with wake-up at 7:00 a.m. At first their son argued, especially on weekends. But after two weeks, mornings were smoother. He needed fewer reminders to get dressed, and his teacher noticed he was calmer during the first lesson of the day. Predictability gave his brain the energy and balance it had been missing.

You can make the same change at home by:

- Choosing a realistic bedtime that gives your child the recommended hours of sleep.

- Holding that bedtime steady every night, even on Fridays and Saturdays.

- Keeping wake-up consistent too, reinforcing it with natural light—open curtains or step outside together.

Children may push back at first, but your consistency is the anchor. Each night you keep the time firm, you're helping their body adjust. Within weeks, mornings feel less frantic and afternoons less volatile.

Think of this regular schedule as an invisible structure. It doesn't rely on charts, rituals, or words—it simply sets the rails that the rest of the day runs on. Other strategies will address what happens during bedtime routines or how to make those moments calmer. Here, the power lies in the clock itself.

Consistency in sleep schedule builds energy and focus.

Strategy 2: Create A Calming Bedtime Routine

Evenings often carry leftover energy. A child may still be bouncing after a day of stimulation, their body unable to switch gears. Without a transition, that restlessness spills straight into bedtime, stretching the night long past the moment when sleep should come.

A calming routine gives the body a clear signal: it's time to slow down. This is not about preparing for school or household routines—only about calming steps that prepare the body for rest. The aim is to choose a few simple actions that lower intensity and repeat them in the same order each night.

One family began with three sensory cues. Their son took a warm bath, slipped into soft pajamas, and then listened to the same gentle song while the lights were dimmed. At first, he still fidgeted in bed, but after a week his body seemed to recognize the sequence. By the time the song began, his breathing slowed and he settled more easily into sleep.

You can shape your own version with soothing signals such as:

- Warm water to relax muscles.
- A low light source that softens the room.

- Quiet background sounds like a short playlist of soft music or white noise.

- A brief physical wind-down such as light stretching or slow breathing.

The routine works because the body begins to expect it. Each night the repeated signals—heat, dim light, steady rhythm—train the nervous system to shift into rest mode. Over time, this predictability turns evenings from battles into smoother landings.

Predictable calm leads to restful sleep.

Strategy 3: Limit Screen Time Before Bed

This strategy focuses only on evening screen habits related to sleep, not daytime technology rules. The goal is to reduce the stimulation that keeps the brain awake long after the lights are turned off.

Many children with ADHD find screens magnetic. The fast-moving images, bright colors, and constant novelty make it almost impossible to turn away. At night, though, that stimulation works against rest. The blue light from tablets, TVs, and phones delays the body's natural release of melatonin, keeping the brain alert just when it should be winding down.

A simple household rule, no screens in the hour before bed, can make a major difference. By cutting off electronic use early, you reduce both the light exposure and the mental excitement that keep your child wired late into the night.

One family decided that all devices would be switched off by 8:00 p.m. At first, their daughter protested, insisting she couldn't fall asleep without watching her favorite show. The parents stayed firm and replaced the last half-hour with puzzles and coloring. Within a week, her bedtime resistance eased. She was not only falling asleep faster but also waking in a better mood, no longer groggy and irritable in the morning.

You can make this shift easier by planning clear alternatives:

- Board or card games that last 15–20 minutes

- Quiet creative activities like drawing or simple crafts

- Reading together in bed or letting your child flip through picture books

Consistency matters. If the rule changes from night to night, children quickly learn to argue. But when the expectation is steady, with screens off at the same time and replaced with calmer activities, the body adapts. Parents often notice not just better sleep but fewer evening meltdowns as overstimulation fades.

Turning off screens turns on sleep.

Strategy 4: Create A Sleep Friendly Bedroom

Beyond routines and rituals, the bedroom itself matters. The physical environment can either help the body drift into rest or keep it on high alert. For children with ADHD, a room that is too bright, noisy, or crowded with distractions makes it harder to settle, no matter how good the routine leading up to bed may be.

Think of the space as a cue. When the bedroom feels dark, quiet, and orderly, the brain receives the message that it is time to sleep. When toys are scattered within reach or outside noise filters through thin curtains, the signal gets blurred.

One family discovered that their son kept waking up to streetlights shining in through the window. After installing blackout curtains and adding a small, warm night-light, he began sleeping more soundly. Another family noticed that bedtime stalling often began with "just one more toy." They moved bins of playthings into another room, and the nightly arguments disappeared. A third parent introduced a white noise machine to cover sudden sounds from neighbors, and their daughter stopped jumping awake at every bark or car horn.

You can improve your child's sleep environment with small, practical changes such as:

- Use blackout curtains or shades to block outside light.

- Provide a soft night-light if complete darkness causes anxiety.

- Remove stimulating toys or store them out of sight.

- Keep the room tidy so the bed becomes the clear center of attention.

- Add calming sound, like a fan or white noise, to smooth out background disturbances.

These adjustments don't need to be expensive or complicated. Each one reduces stimulation and strengthens the association between the bedroom and sleep. Over time, the room itself becomes part of the signal that helps your child's body settle more quickly.

The right environment makes falling asleep easier.

Strategy 5: Provide Balanced Meals At Regular Times

Children with ADHD often swing between bursts of energy and sudden crashes. Skipping meals or eating at irregular times makes those ups and downs sharper. A steady rhythm of meals and snacks smooths the day, giving the body the predictability it needs to regulate mood and attention.

The focus here is timing. When food arrives at consistent intervals, energy stays more even. Long gaps without eating can lead to irritability, restlessness, and difficulty focusing. A reliable schedule prevents those sudden dips and helps children feel more in control of their bodies.

One family noticed that their daughter often had emotional meltdowns in the late afternoon. Looking back, they realized she was skipping breakfast and sometimes forgetting to eat lunch at school. They set a pattern of three meals and two snacks at regular times.

Within days, her afternoon behavior improved. She still had challenges with homework, but the explosive irritability that used to show up before dinner was far less frequent.

You can set the rhythm in simple ways:

- Keep breakfast, lunch, and dinner at roughly the same hours each day
- Add one snack mid-morning and one mid-afternoon
- Maintain the pattern on weekends and holidays so the body doesn't lose the rhythm
- Avoid long stretches without food, especially before demanding activities like school or sports

The foods themselves will be addressed in other strategies. Here, the emphasis is on consistency. Just as a steady bedtime helps the body expect sleep, a steady meal schedule helps the body expect nourishment. When eating becomes predictable, energy is more stable and children are better able to focus on what the day requires of them.

Food is fuel for focus.

Strategy 6: Limit Sugary Snacks And Drinks

For children with ADHD, sugar works like a switch that flips energy on and off too quickly. A soda or a candy bar might bring a short burst of excitement, but soon after comes the crash—fatigue, irritability, and difficulty concentrating. When these ups and downs repeat through the day, behavior and focus become harder to manage.

This strategy is not about when meals happen or how to balance nutrients. It is only about cutting back on high-sugar foods and replacing them with options that keep energy steadier.

One family realized their son's daily tantrums almost always began after he grabbed cookies with a sugary drink in the afternoon. They swapped them for a fruit smoothie and some popcorn. The first days brought complaints, but after a week he was calmer at homework time, and the cycle of late-afternoon meltdowns eased.

You can make the same shift by offering alternatives such as:

- Fresh fruit or fruit smoothies
- Yogurt with a drizzle of honey instead of candy
- Light popcorn instead of chips or cookies
- Whole-grain granola bars instead of chocolate bars

Children still need treats, but when sweets stop being the everyday fuel, they lose their destabilizing effect. Ice cream at a weekend outing or cake at a birthday party feels special without throwing off daily rhythms.

Less sugar, more steady energy. And when desserts turn into occasional celebrations rather than constant snacks, they become moments of joy instead of obstacles to balance.

Strategy 7: Include Protein In Every Meal

Protein works like a steady fuel for the brain. For children with ADHD, it smooths out energy levels so they can stay alert and calmer for longer periods. A small source of protein at each meal gives their body something solid to rely on instead of the short bursts that come from foods that burn off too quickly.

This strategy is only about adding protein. It is not about sugar or meal timing, which are covered elsewhere. The focus here is simple: make sure every plate includes a protein source.

One parent noticed her son came home restless after school. Lunch usually meant pasta or bread, and teachers reported he was fidgety all afternoon. She began packing a small yogurt or a few slices of chicken with his meal. The difference was clear. He was steadier through the afternoon and less irritable at homework time.

Everyday options can be quick and practical:

- Scrambled or hard-boiled eggs

- Yogurt or cottage cheese

- A spoonful of peanut butter on toast

- Slices of turkey, chicken, or tuna

- Beans, lentils, or hummus spread on crackers

The aim is not elaborate meals but regularity. Even one spoonful of nut butter or a slice of turkey in a sandwich can shift your child's focus for the rest of the afternoon.

Protein at every meal keeps the body fueled and gives the brain the stability it needs.

Strategy 8: Schedule Daily Physical Activity

Children with ADHD often have energy that needs a regular outlet. Without daily movement, that energy builds up and shows itself as restlessness, short tempers, or difficulty concentrating. Setting aside time to be active every day works like a natural reset, helping your child stay calmer during the day and settle more easily at night.

This strategy is not about sports leagues or learning new skills. It is about making sure there is a block of time, at least thirty to sixty minutes, where your child's body can move freely and consistently.

One family noticed their son grew irritable whenever he spent the day indoors. They committed to half an hour of movement no matter the weather. Some days it was a short bike ride, other days it was dancing in the living room. Within a week, his evenings grew smoother. He was not suddenly eager for bed, but the nightly resistance faded because his body had already released some of its tension.

You can build this outlet with simple, flexible options:

- A bike or scooter ride around the block

- Quick outdoor games such as tag or catch

- Dancing together to music in the living room

- Jumping rope or bouncing a ball

- Light stretching before bedtime to relax the body

What matters most is not the kind of activity but its regularity. Indoors or outdoors, alone or with others, the body learns to expect that time each day. That rhythm reduces hyperactivity, steadies mood, and helps evenings unfold with less conflict.

Daily movement gives your child the release they need so energy does not spill into arguments or frustration.

Strategy 9: Try Relaxation Techniques Before Sleep

Even with a good routine and a sleep-friendly bedroom, many children with ADHD struggle to switch off at night. Their minds stay busy, their bodies fidget, and the more they try to "just fall asleep," the harder it becomes. Gentle relaxation techniques can help bridge that gap, giving both body and mind a way to ease into rest.

This strategy is not about bedtime rituals or words of comfort. It focuses on simple, physical methods that lower tension and signal the nervous system to slow down.

One parent began guiding her son through five slow breaths each night. At first he resisted, saying it was boring, but after a week he started to ask for it. She noticed that instead of lying awake for an hour, he now fell asleep within minutes. Another family added light stretching before pajamas. Their daughter, who used to toss and turn, settled faster once her muscles felt relaxed.

You can experiment with small practices such as:

- Deep breathing: ask your child to place a hand on their belly and feel it rise and fall with each breath

- Gentle stretching: a few slow movements to release tension from legs and shoulders

- Soft background music: quiet rhythms or white noise that help the body let go of alertness

The goal isn't perfection but consistency. Even two or three minutes of relaxation before bed can reset the body and make sleep easier. Over time, these signals become a nightly cue, helping your child leave behind the day's stimulation.

Relaxation closes the day peacefully.

Strategy 10: Involve Your Child In Healthy Choices

Children are more willing to follow healthy habits when they take part in shaping them. If every decision about food or movement comes from adults alone, resistance grows. When children are invited to choose within clear limits, cooperation feels easier.

One family had daily battles over snacks. Their son pushed back whenever fruit was placed in front of him. At the grocery store, his parents began offering a choice between apples or grapes. At home he ate the fruit he had picked himself, and the arguments disappeared. Another parent gave her daughter the option of a short bike ride or a walk to the park. Because she had a say, she embraced the activity instead of resisting it.

You can create the same opportunities in everyday life:

- Offer a choice between two healthy snacks.

- Let your child decide which playground or park to visit.

- Invite them to help prepare food by washing fruit or arranging items on a plate.

The key is to keep both options healthy and realistic. Your child feels involved, but the direction remains in your hands. Over time, these small decisions build a sense of ownership. Healthy eating and daily movement begin to feel like personal preferences rather than rules imposed from above.

When children participate in choices about food and activity, healthy habits take root more naturally and last longer.

Chapter 8:
Strategies To Set Healthy Limits On Technology Use

"Technology is a useful servant but a dangerous master." —
Christian Lous Lange

E vening arguments over screens are familiar in many homes. Your child has been playing a video game for hours, and when you say it's time to stop, the response is a sharp "No!" followed by tears or shouting. The same pattern might appear with YouTube, television, or a tablet. What begins as entertainment often ends in conflict, with you feeling like the "bad guy" for pulling the plug. The longer it goes on, the more tense the house becomes—bedtime gets delayed, siblings complain, and you're left drained from the battle.

Technology itself is not the enemy. Devices help your child learn, connect, and relax. But without clear limits, they can consume the day, leaving less time for physical play, creative activities, or even basic rest. Many children with ADHD find it especially difficult to self-regulate with screens. The fast pace, bright visuals, and constant novelty pull them in so strongly that stopping feels impossible. Without rules, the result is often irritability, sleep struggles, and endless negotiations.

Now imagine the same situation with a small but powerful change. A family decides that screen time will always end at the same hour, no exceptions. A timer is set, and when it rings, the device powers off automatically. At first, their son protests, but after a week he begins to expect it. The tantrums shrink, bedtime moves smoothly, and the rest of the evening is calmer. The parents no longer feel like policemen—they feel like guides who created a system that works.

That contrast is the reason this chapter exists. You don't need to ban technology or turn your home into a battlefield. You need strategies that make boundaries predictable, enforceable, and fair. With the right structure, devices become one part of life, not the center of it.

In the next pages, you'll find ten strategies designed for real families, not perfect ones. You'll learn how to set daily limits that children understand, create tech-free spaces at home, and use parental controls without constant arguing. You'll see how to replace screen time with alternatives that actually interest your child, and how to turn devices into privileges earned through cooperation rather than automatic rights. You'll also discover simple ways to involve your child in the process, making them more likely to respect the rules instead of resisting them.

Each strategy is specific and practical. For example, one family cut daily battles in half by posting a weekly screen schedule on a whiteboard where everyone could see it. Another found that replacing evening tablet time with a short board game reduced whining and gave the children something to look forward to. These aren't miracles—they are small systems that prevent chaos and bring back balance.

As you read, keep in mind that no two children respond in the same way. A rule that works in one household may need adjusting in another. The point is not perfection, but progress. Each step you take reduces conflict, protects family connection, and teaches your child that technology is a tool, not a trap.

By the end of this chapter, you'll have a toolkit of strategies that help screens fit into your family life without taking it over. Technology will still be part of your child's world, but it will no longer dictate the rhythm of your days. The power struggles will shrink, your evenings will open up, and your child will grow up learning one of the most important lessons for life in the digital age: how to use technology without being ruled by it.

Strategy 1: Set Clear Daily Screen Time Limits

This strategy is about the total daily amount of screen time, not about when in the evening screens are turned off—that is covered elsewhere. The focus here is on defining how many minutes or hours per day are allowed, so screens stay a part of life without taking over.

Children with ADHD often lose track of time when using devices. What feels like "just five more minutes" can quickly stretch into an hour or more. When no boundary exists, conflict begins the moment you ask them to stop. A clear daily limit removes the uncertainty. Everyone knows how long screens are available, and once the time is up, there is no room for debate.

A practical range is one to two hours per day, divided into shorter sessions. The exact number can shift depending on your child's age and your family rhythm, but the key is consistency. If the rule changes every day, you'll end up negotiating constantly. If it stays steady, children learn to expect it and plan around it.

One family created a simple rule: thirty minutes after school and thirty minutes after dinner. Their son was free to choose what to watch or play, but when the timer rang, the device was put away. At first he resisted, but within weeks he started asking, "How many minutes do I have left?" instead of begging for more time. The predictability made the transition easier for everyone.

Here are three ways to make this system work:

- Set the total limit clearly. Decide in advance how many minutes or hours per day are allowed.

- Use a timer only to end screen time. The alarm marks the stop, not the structure of daily routines (covered elsewhere) and not to teach self-monitoring—that will come in a later strategy.

- Make the rule visible. Write the daily limit on a chart or whiteboard so there is no confusion.

This strategy is different from others in this chapter. It is not about posting schedules (that comes later) and not about teaching your child to self-regulate with timers (that is another step). Here, the parent defines the maximum amount of daily screen time and sticks to it.

When children know exactly how much time they have, they can enjoy their devices without constant arguments. And when the limit is reached, the rule—not your mood—ends the session.

Clear limits prevent endless battles over screens.

Strategy 2: Create Tech Free Zones At Home

Unlike strategies that focus on how much time children spend on screens, this one is only about where devices are not allowed. The goal is to protect specific household spaces so they remain tied to family life instead of technology.

When screens show up everywhere — at the dinner table, on the couch, or in bedrooms — they begin to dominate the atmosphere. For children with ADHD, this constant availability makes it even harder to pause and shift to other activities. Setting clear tech free zones gives structure to the environment itself, turning places in the house into natural reminders that not every moment belongs to a device.

The dinner table is often the easiest place to start. A simple rule such as "No screens at meals" turns eating into a chance for connection instead of distraction. Bedrooms can also benefit from this approach. Bedrooms stay calmer when they are places for rest instead of screens, and making them device free during the day prevents them from turning into another gaming or video space. Some families also pick the car as a zone without screens, which turns short rides into opportunities for music, conversation, or even quiet time.

To make this practical:

- Choose two or three spaces where screens are always off limits.

- Keep the rule clear and consistent, for example: "No screens at meals."

- Offer alternatives that fit the context, like conversation at the table or an audiobook in the car.

This strategy is different from limits on daily screen time and different from planning family activities without technology. The focus here is spatial and everyday — fixed household spots that remain screen free regardless of schedule or events.

When children learn that certain spots in the house never involve screens, those places naturally invite conversation, play, or quiet time. Tech free zones anchor parts of your home in real interaction.

Strategy 3: Model Healthy Tech Habits As A Parent

Children notice what you do even more than what you say. With technology, your own habits often set the strongest example. If you check your phone throughout dinner, it is hard to convince your child to keep theirs away. If you scroll in bed at night, they will wonder why the same behavior is off-limits for them.

Modeling healthy tech habits means showing balance in your daily choices. It is about demonstrating that devices can be part of life without taking control of it.

One mother realized her son ignored the rule about no screens at dinner because she often checked her work emails at the table. When she began leaving her phone in another room during meals, the conflict stopped. Another parent used to watch television late into the night and struggled to convince his daughter to turn hers off. By switching to reading a short book before bed, he improved his own sleep and gave his daughter a clear example of how to end the day without screens.

You can model balance in simple ways:

- Put your phone away during meals and family moments.
- Turn off notifications in the evening so screens do not interrupt rest.
- Choose offline activities such as reading, cooking, or talking where your child can see real alternatives in action.

Modeling focuses on your own behavior. By treating devices as tools to be managed rather than constant companions, you show your child what balance looks like in practice. Over time, your actions create a quiet but steady rule in the house: technology fits into life without controlling it.

Strategy 4: Use Parental Controls To Enforce Limits

Even when rules are clear, enforcing them can turn into daily arguments. Children with ADHD often push boundaries, and asking them to stop mid-game or leave a favorite app can trigger big reactions. Parental controls help take some of the conflict out of your hands by letting the device itself apply the rule.

The limit still comes from you. The tool simply enforces it automatically, so you don't have to argue each time. This is not about deciding how much screen time your child has — that belongs to the parent. It is about making sure the agreed limit is carried out without repeated negotiations.

Most modern devices include built-in settings to set time caps, block certain content, or pause access after a specific number of minutes. External apps can extend these features across multiple devices in the home. The benefit isn't that technology "babysits," but that it keeps your boundary consistent and predictable.

One family used to fight whenever their son reached the end of his allowed gaming session. He would bargain, complain, and often sneak back onto the console. By setting the console to shut off after the allotted time, the arguments stopped. The rule didn't change — but now the device, not the parent's voice, marked the end.

To use parental controls effectively:

- Match the tool to your rule. If your limit is one hour a day, set the device to lock after sixty minutes.

- Keep it transparent. Show your child how the control works so it doesn't feel like a trick.

- Pair it with conversation. The tool enforces the rule, but your words explain why it exists.

This strategy is different from setting daily limits (Strategy 1), because it is not about defining the boundary. It is about keeping the rule steady once you have decided on it. Unlike tech free zones or modeling, it doesn't change space or behavior — it provides technical backup.

When children see that the device enforces the limit the same way every time, the power struggle shrinks. Technology doesn't replace your rules, it makes them constant and fair.

Strategy 5: Replace Screen Time With Engaging Alternatives

Telling a child with ADHD to "just stop using the tablet" rarely works. When a device is removed without something else to fill the gap, boredom and frustration take over, and conflict quickly follows. The smoother path is to swap screens with activities that are interesting enough to capture attention on their own.

This isn't about setting daily screen time rules or planning big family outings. It's about everyday swaps that make the non-screen option just as inviting. The goal is to create choices that are ready, visible, and easy to access in the moment.

One family noticed their daughter demanded the TV every afternoon as soon as she got home. Instead of arguing, they placed a basket of quick board games near the living room. After school, she could pick one to play with a parent or sibling before turning to screens. The new routine reduced whining because the alternative felt fun, not like punishment.

You can prepare the same effect at home by keeping alternatives within easy reach:

- Hands-on games. Board games, card games, puzzles, or building sets.

- Creative activities. Drawing, crafts, baking cookies, or building a fort with cushions.

- Movement indoors. Short dance sessions, balloon volleyball, or a scavenger hunt around the house.

The key is preparation. If you wait until your child is already demanding the tablet, the argument is harder to win. But when another option is already in sight, the transition feels natural.

When children discover that screen time isn't the only exciting choice, turning off devices stops feeling like the end of fun. When a board game is already on the table or a puzzle box is waiting nearby, saying yes to play becomes easier than fighting over screens.

Strategy 6: Create A Screen Time Schedule Visible To All

Even when screen limits are clear, children may still ask "When can I watch?" or "Can I play now?" ten times a day. For a child with ADHD, that uncertainty fuels conflict. A visible schedule takes the guessing out. Everyone knows when screen time happens, and the plan speaks louder than arguments.

One family kept a whiteboard in the kitchen. They wrote 4:00–4:30 as video game time and 7:00–7:30 as family TV. Whenever their son asked, "Is it time yet?" they pointed to the board. The questions stopped, because the answer was always there. Another family used a simple weekly chart on paper taped to the fridge. By seeing which days had longer or shorter sessions, their daughter felt the system was fair and predictable.

The goal here isn't to debate how long screens are allowed, but to make the plan visible so children can follow it without constant reminders.

To make this practical:

- Choose simple, stable tools. A wall calendar, paper chart, or whiteboard works best.

- Mark clear blocks of time. Use easy labels like "after snack" or "7–7:30 PM."

- Place it in plain sight. The fridge or a family room wall helps everyone see it without asking.

Keep in mind that this schedule is only for screens, not for household routines or schoolwork. Its purpose is to give children a clear reference point so you don't need to repeat yourself.

Instead of asking you again, your child can glance at the chart and know exactly when their turn comes.

Strategy 7: Teach Self Monitoring With Timers

How do you help a child stop screen time without turning it into an argument? For many families, this is the hardest part of managing devices. A timer can provide structure, not by forcing a shutdown, but by teaching your child to notice time passing and respond independently.

Self monitoring means that your child begins to link the signal of the timer with their own decision to stop. At first, the cue comes from the outside. Over time, it becomes a tool they use for themselves, shifting the control from you to them.

One father introduced a visual timer shaped like a traffic light. As the green section faded into yellow, his son began preparing to turn off the console. Soon he was announcing, "I have two minutes left," and shutting it down without reminders. The timer had become his own tool for regulation.

You can try the same approach with simple steps:

- Choose a timer that is easy to read, such as a sand timer, a traffic-light style visual timer, or a kitchen alarm with sound or color.

- Stay nearby in the beginning and reinforce the action when the signal appears.

- Step back gradually so your child learns to respond without your prompting.

Reserve this tool for screen time so it remains clear and specific. Each time your child turns off the device after the timer rings, they experience more than compliance. They feel the confidence of managing technology by themselves, an important step toward real self control.

Strategy 8: Encourage Outdoor Time Before Screen Time

For many children with ADHD, screens are so engaging that once they start, it's almost impossible to stop. By setting a rule that outdoor play comes first, you ensure their body gets movement before their mind dives into digital stimulation. The focus here is not on how long they play outside, but on making outdoor time the gateway to screens.

One family decided that after school, their son had to spend at least 30 minutes outdoors before turning on the TV. At first he resisted, but soon he accepted the sequence: ride the bike first, then relax with cartoons. Another family used the backyard trampoline. Their daughter knew that a short bouncing session came before video games. With her energy already released, arguments about turning the console on disappeared.

To put this into practice:

- Set a clear minimum. Even 20 minutes of outdoor time creates the pattern.

- Keep choices simple. A ball, scooter, swing, or walking the dog is enough.

- Stick to the sequence. Outdoor activity always comes first, no exceptions.

When outdoor play is the natural ticket to screen time, children stop fighting the rule because they know what comes next. Shoes off after the backyard run, then the remote comes out — and there's no fight about what comes first.

Strategy 9: Use Screen Time As A Privilege Earned By Cooperation

When children see screens as a right, every limit feels unfair. By shifting the perspective to privilege, you change the tone: access to technology becomes something earned through cooperation, not something automatically granted.

For children with ADHD, this link works well because screens are the currency they value most. When used carefully, that currency becomes a clear and motivating way to connect positive behavior with access to what they enjoy.

One family tied screen time to cooperation during household routines. Their son earned 20 minutes of play by clearing the table without protests. Another family used the same principle for respectful communication: when their daughter handled a disagreement calmly, she received her evening show as recognition. In both cases, the message was the same — cooperation opens the door to screens.

To make this practical:

- State the rule clearly. "Screen time is something you earn when you cooperate."

- Link it to everyday cooperation. Helping with chores, transitioning without arguing, or showing respectful words.

- Keep it positive and immediate. The privilege works best when granted soon after the cooperative act.

This isn't about punishment or threats. It's not removing screens because of misbehavior — it's granting them as a privilege in response to positive action. Keep the focus narrow: screens are the reward, nothing else.

Screens are the currency your child understands best — keep this link to cooperation only in the context of technology. When children learn that cooperation unlocks screen time, arguments shrink and the family atmosphere shifts toward teamwork instead of battles.

Strategy 10: Plan Regular Tech Free Family Activities

When was the last time your family spent an evening together without phones, tablets, or television? Screens often pull everyone into separate corners: one child gaming, another watching videos, and a parent scrolling. Planning tech free moments gives your family a chance to share space again and helps your child see that some of the best memories are made without devices.

These activities are not about individual limits or strict rules. They are about building regular times when everyone sets screens aside and attention shifts back to people.

One family created a Friday board game night. At first their son resisted, but soon he was excited to choose the game and laugh through the rounds. Another family began Sunday afternoon walks. With phones left at home, those walks turned into a predictable time for conversation and fun.

You can plan the same kind of activities in simple ways:

- Choose a format that fits your family, such as board games, cooking together, a short walk, or a creative project.

- Keep it predictable by picking a day or time and repeating it so it becomes part of the week.

- Give your child a voice by letting them help choose the activity.

The strength of these activities comes from their consistency. When children know that certain times always belong to family life and not to screens, they begin to expect them and often look forward to them. Over time, these shared offline moments become anchors of connection that balance the strong pull of technology.

Chapter 9: Strategies To Nurture Family Relationships And Sibling Bonds

"The memories we make with our family are everything." —
Candace Cameron Bure

I t starts with a fight over something small. One child wants the blue marker, the other grabs it first. Voices rise, arms flail, and within seconds the living room turns into a battlefield. For a child with ADHD, whose impulses fire quickly and intensely, these moments can spark daily clashes. Their sibling, who may already feel overlooked because so much attention goes toward managing ADHD, reacts with frustration of their own. What could have been a quiet afternoon of drawing together ends with slammed doors and heavy silence.

Tensions like these leave more than noise behind. Over time, constant conflicts can plant seeds of jealousy and distance. The sibling without ADHD may start to think, *"Mom always steps in for him, but never for me."* The child with ADHD may feel ganged up on, convinced that no one understands their side. Left unchecked, these dynamics chip away at family harmony. Instead of companionship, siblings become rivals. Instead of laughter, shared time turns into a cycle of irritation and hurt feelings.

But the story can unfold differently. Picture the same two children a week later. The markers are on the table again, but this time, before frustration has a chance to grow, their parent reminds them of a clear family rule: "Ask before borrowing." The child with ADHD pauses, asks for the blue one, and the sibling hands it over without a fight. A few minutes later, they're bent over the same paper, laughing as they add silly shapes to each other's drawings. What once erupted into conflict now becomes a small but joyful memory.

Moments like this don't appear out of luck. They happen because parents set the stage for connection—by creating rituals that bring siblings together, setting rules that prevent disrespect, and carving out individual time so each child feels seen. With clear strategies, family life shifts from constant fire-fighting to a space where bonds grow steadily stronger.

Think of a family movie night. In the past, arguments over who chose last time might have ended with one sibling storming off. After a parent introduced a ritual where each child takes turns picking, the tension eased. Friday nights turned into an event everyone looked forward to, complete with popcorn, blankets, and inside jokes that carried into the week. That change wasn't about removing ADHD from the picture—it was about shaping family life in a way that made room for everyone.

This chapter will guide you through ten practical strategies to help you create more of those positive moments. You'll learn how to balance the scales of attention with one-on-one time, set clear rules for respect that siblings can actually follow, and teach conflict resolution skills that turn arguments into problem-solving opportunities. You'll explore ways to build rituals of togetherness, explain ADHD to siblings in age-appropriate terms, and create opportunities for teamwork that reduce rivalry. You'll also see how fairness in praise, protection of personal space, and healthy roles for older siblings protect family harmony. And finally, you'll discover how making family memories—both big and small—anchors your children in a sense of belonging that lasts.

These strategies are not abstract theories. They are small, repeatable moves that shift the daily tone inside your home. A short walk with one child, a poster on the wall with three simple rules, a weekly game night, or a gentle reminder that ADHD behaviors come from a different brain, not from "doing it on purpose"—each step changes the way your children see each other. Over time, these steps add up to something far more powerful than the absence of fights. They create a foundation of respect, laughter, and trust that siblings carry with them for years.

By the end of this chapter, you'll have a toolkit designed to strengthen family relationships and ease sibling rivalry. The goal is not perfection or a home without conflict—arguments will still happen. The goal is to guide those moments so they don't define your family life. What defines it, instead, are the stories your children will remember: the evenings of shared pizza, the laughter during board games, the bedtime rituals where everyone felt included. These memories become the glue that holds siblings together, even on hard days, and the foundation that helps your family grow stronger, not more divided, because of ADHD.

Strategy 1: Schedule One On One Time With Each Child

When a child with ADHD draws much of the household's energy, siblings often feel left in the shadows. They may not complain out loud, but they notice the imbalance. Over time, that sense of being overlooked can turn into jealousy, frustration, or distance. The goal of one-on-one time is not only to strengthen your bond with each child, but to show them that attention is shared fairly among all members of the family.

These moments don't need to be long or elaborate. Fifteen to twenty minutes of undivided presence is enough to reassure a sibling that they have their own space with you. A short ice cream run, a walk around the block, or simply closing the door to play a quick card game after dinner tells them, *"You matter just as much, and I see you."*

One mother noticed her daughter pulling away whenever homework time focused on her brother with ADHD. The girl wasn't struggling academically, but she felt invisible in those hours. To counterbalance, they created "milkshake night"—a short weekly ritual where the two of them walked to the corner café, just the two of them. Within weeks, the sulking eased. The girl opened up more about her day, and her attitude toward her brother softened because she no longer felt overshadowed.

Another parent started small "mini dates" with each child on weekends. Sometimes it was a bike ride, sometimes ten minutes of cards in their room after dinner. These brief slices of attention shifted the family dynamic: instead of tallying who got more of Mom or Dad, the children began to expect and appreciate their own turn.

To make this work at home:

- Keep the time short and predictable—15–20 minutes per child is enough.

- Protect it from interruptions: put the phone away and give full focus.

- Let each child know when their turn is, so anticipation replaces resentment.

These moments aren't about pampering one child or giving them "special treatment." They are about balance. When every child knows they will have time alone with you, the pressure eases, rivalry fades, and family bonds grow stronger.

Strategy 2: Set Clear Rules For Respect Among Siblings

Brothers and sisters spend hours together—playing, sharing space, borrowing each other's things. In families with ADHD, those everyday moments can tip quickly into shouting or pushing if boundaries aren't crystal clear. These aren't household-wide behavior rules about manners or chores; they are simple agreements designed only for siblings, to guide how they treat one another in play and in daily life.

One family with three children kept running into the same problem: their son with ADHD would burst into his sister's room and grab her markers without asking. She would yell, he would snap back, and soon both were in tears. Their parents sat down with the kids and created a short list of "sibling respect rules." They kept it simple and specific:

- Ask before borrowing
- No entering each other's rooms without permission
- No insults or name-calling during play

The rules went on a colorful poster taped near the hallway where everyone could see them. The next time the sister saw her brother reaching for her markers, she didn't scream. She pointed at the poster and said, "Remember—ask first." It didn't end every quarrel, but it gave both children a neutral way to settle small clashes before they exploded.

To make this work in your home:

- Keep the list short—three or four rules at most.
- Write them in positive, easy-to-repeat language.
- Focus them only on sibling interactions: toys, rooms, words, play.
- Place them somewhere visible so children can point to them when needed.

Respect rules between siblings aren't about discipline or punishment. They're a shared code that makes daily life feel fair. When each child knows what's expected in games, conversations, and shared spaces, jealousy fades and bonds have room to grow.

Strategy 3: Teach Conflict Resolution Skills At Home

Siblings argue—it's part of growing up together. But when ADHD adds impulsivity and quick tempers, those everyday disagreements can spin out of control. The goal here isn't to stop conflict altogether. It's to give your children a simple way to move through it so arguments don't turn into bruised feelings or broken trust. This approach is meant only for sibling clashes at home—sharing toys, taking turns, deciding who gets the bigger slice of pizza—not for school or friendships outside the family.

One father noticed his sons would explode every time they both wanted the same video game controller. He introduced a short, four-step routine just for sibling disputes:

1. Stop – Pause and put the item down.

2. Calm down – Count to five or take a breath.

3. Listen – Each sibling says what they want.

4. Take turns talking – No interrupting until the other is finished.

At first, he walked them through each step. Soon enough, the boys began using the words themselves—"My turn to talk!"—and arguments turned into quicker, calmer negotiations.

A mother applied the same routine when her daughters fought over the front seat in the car. They practiced the steps, and within weeks the girls started settling it themselves: "You go today, I'll go tomorrow."

Even small flashpoints can benefit. Two brothers once clashed daily about who used the bathroom first in the morning. After practicing the same four steps, they worked out a rotation without their mom needing to step in.

You can make this work best by practicing in calm moments, maybe role-playing with a toy or a pretend scenario, so the steps feel natural when real tension flares. Keep your language short and simple—"Take turns talking," "Count to five"—so it feels like guidance, not a lecture.

When children learn to resolve arguments this way, they don't just stop yelling. They discover that fights over toys, turns, or space can end with solutions, and sometimes even laughter.

Strategy 4: Create Family Rituals Of Togetherness

Family life can feel scattered by homework battles, sibling arguments, and last-minute rushes. Setting regular rituals brings back a rhythm everyone can count on and reminds children that there is time each week reserved for being together.

These rituals are not about celebrating one child or creating private signals. They are moments for the whole family, repeated often enough that they become part of the household rhythm.

One family chose Friday pizza night. Each person had a role—rolling dough, adding toppings, setting the table. By the time the pizza came out of the oven, the room was full of chatter and laughter, and the evening carried the feeling of unity. Another family built the habit of Sunday afternoon walks. Rain or shine, the children grew to expect it, and the predictability made it something they looked forward to.

You can keep these rituals simple and sustainable:

- Pancake mornings where everyone stirs the batter in turn.
- A weekly board game after dinner.
- Reading a chapter aloud together before bed on weekends.

The power lies in consistency. These shared practices send a clear message: family time is protected and everyone belongs. Even when the day has been filled with disagreements, the ritual itself stays steady and gives siblings a chance to reconnect.

Over time, these traditions become anchors. Long after the details fade, your children will remember the feeling of Friday night laughter or Sunday walks as proof that family life always included space for togetherness.

Strategy 5: Teach Siblings About ADHD In Age-Appropriate Ways

Siblings see everything. They notice when their brother blurts out answers before anyone else, when their sister forgets the rules of a game, or when one child gets more reminders and patience from parents. Without context, it's easy for them to think, *"He's cheating,"* or *"She always gets away with it."* These thoughts, left unspoken, can quietly harden into resentment.

Clear, simple explanations help. When siblings understand that ADHD is part of how their brother or sister's brain works—not a choice to be unfair—they start seeing the behavior differently. One mother explained to her daughter, "His brain is like trying to play a game with music blasting in the background. He really wants to follow the rules, but it's harder to stay on track." The next time her brother forgot a turn, instead of yelling, she reminded him gently and the game kept going.

You don't need long talks or complicated science. For younger children, you might say: *"Her brain works like a busy road, with too many cars trying to go at once."* For older ones: *"ADHD makes it harder to focus and stop impulses. It's not that he doesn't care—it's that he needs more practice."* These bite-size explanations make sense in the world children already know.

Real-life examples bring the idea home. One father noticed his oldest son was furious every time his younger brother broke Lego structures. After learning that impulsivity made it hard for his sibling to pause, he began setting aside sturdier pieces for them to build together. The frustration didn't disappear, but blame softened into teamwork.

Practical ways to share this understanding with siblings:

- Keep it short and familiar—use everyday comparisons they already grasp.

- Repeat explanations as needed, because a single talk isn't enough.

- Tie the explanation to what they actually experience at home, like games, turns, or shared projects.

That shift doesn't erase sibling clashes, but it changes the tone. Instead of shouting or assuming bad intentions, children become more likely to step in with help, reminders, or patience.

Strategy 6: Give Siblings Opportunities To Work As A Team

Rivalry grows when children feel like opponents. One wins, the other loses, and the scoreboard of daily life tilts back and forth. You can soften that competition by giving siblings chances to work on the same side. When they succeed together—whether in the kitchen, the yard, or the living room—they stop seeing each other only as rivals and start experiencing what it feels like to be a team.

A mother of two boys used to hear constant bickering about who was "better" at everything. She began inviting them to help with Sunday pancakes: one cracked eggs while the other mixed batter. By the time the stack was ready, the boys were laughing at the lumps instead of competing over who had done more. What mattered wasn't perfect pancakes but that both had a role in making them.

Another family set up a garden project. The older sibling dug holes while the younger carried seedlings. At the end of the afternoon, they stood side by side admiring a row of plants they had both contributed to. That visible result turned into a shared point of pride—something they could water and watch grow together.

Teamwork doesn't need to be tied to big projects. Small, everyday tasks carry the same weight:

- Building a puzzle together at the dining table.

- Decorating cupcakes, each adding a topping before passing the tray along.

- Tidying the living room before guests arrive, with one folding blankets while the other clears the table.

These activities work because the outcome depends on combined effort, not on who finishes first. Each shared success chips away at rivalry and builds trust that brothers and sisters can cooperate.

Over time, these experiences become proof that they can laugh, build, and solve problems on the same side.

Strategy 7: Balance Praise Fairly Among Children

Children keep score, even if they never say it out loud. When one sibling seems to receive more compliments—especially the child with ADHD who may need extra encouragement—the others can feel overlooked. Over time, that imbalance can spark jealousy and quiet resentment.

One mother saw this after praising her son with ADHD for finishing his homework without reminders. His sister, who had just set the table, frowned and muttered, "Nobody ever notices me." The mother adjusted her approach. The next evening she said, "I'm proud of how you both helped today—homework done and table ready." That small shift turned praise into something shared instead of lopsided.

The goal isn't to hand out identical compliments or to keep a tally. It's about making sure each child hears that their contributions matter. When praise is spread fairly across siblings, it sends the message that everyone plays an important role in family life.

Here are simple ways to keep praise balanced:

- Notice different types of effort—patience in a game, helping with chores, sharing toys.
- Use group praise when they've worked together: "I loved how you both cheered when the puzzle was finished."

- Rotate individual recognition so no one feels invisible over time.

One father created a short bedtime ritual: "Tell me one thing you did today that you're proud of, and I'll share something I noticed too." Both children began to look forward to it, not as competition, but as reassurance that their efforts were equally valued.

When each child hears that their part is noticed, jealousy fades and the sense of being on the same team grows stronger.

Strategy 8: Protect Sibling Personal Space And Belongings

Under one roof, everything feels shared—rooms, toys, even favorite spots on the couch. For siblings, especially when ADHD drives impulsive grabbing or barging in, the lack of clear boundaries often sparks some of the loudest fights. Protecting personal space is about giving each child a few "inviolable" things or zones that belong only to them.

One family faced endless tension because their youngest loved rummaging through his sister's drawers. To him, it was curiosity; to her, it felt like constant intrusion. Their parents set up labeled boxes— one for each child's treasures—placed on a high shelf. Those boxes became off-limits unless the owner gave permission. The fights eased almost immediately, because each child finally had a safe place for what mattered most.

Personal space doesn't require separate bedrooms. It can be as simple as:

- A shelf, drawer, or bin marked with each child's name.

- A quiet chair or desk corner that belongs only to one sibling.

- Separate cups or water bottles, so there's no debate about "who used mine."

One father solved daily Lego clashes by giving his sons their own baskets for unfinished builds. Another family agreed on a "knock before entering" rule whenever a bedroom door was closed—even parents followed it. Those small boundaries gave siblings confidence that their things and spaces wouldn't be touched without consent.

When children know their special spots or belongings are safe, everyday life feels calmer—and sharing the rest becomes easier.

Strategy 9: Teach Older Siblings Healthy Support Roles

When a child has ADHD, it's easy for parents to lean on older siblings for help. Over time, though, those requests can start to feel heavy—more like parenting than playing. Brothers and sisters should not be in charge of managing meltdowns or enforcing rules. What works better is giving them small, light ways to join in, so they can feel helpful without carrying the weight of responsibility.

One family noticed their teenage daughter had grown resentful after being told too often to "watch your brother." They shifted her role completely. Instead of monitoring behavior, she was invited to do fun things with him: helping frost cupcakes, teaming up for a puzzle, or teaching him the rules of a new card game. She began to look forward to these moments, because they felt like sibling time—not babysitting.

Another mother stepped in when she saw her older son trying to calm his brother during tantrums. She told him clearly: "That's my job. Your job is just to play." The relief was obvious. Once he knew the pressure wasn't his to carry, he enjoyed being around his brother again.

Here are a few ways older siblings can join in without feeling like caretakers:

- Reading a page or two aloud before bedtime.
- Showing how to stack chairs after dinner.

- Guiding a younger sibling through the first round of a board game.

- Helping stir pancake batter or decorate a cupcake.

These gestures are short, playful, and rooted in everyday family life. They don't ask the older sibling to take charge—just to share a skill or a moment.

When support stays playful and light, siblings see each other as teammates, not caretakers.

Strategy 10: Create Positive Family Memories Regularly

Daily life can get crowded with corrections, chores, and sibling quarrels. What cuts through the noise are the experiences that stand out—moments that feel different from the routine and turn into stories children carry with them. Creating these memories doesn't require grand vacations. Small but special family experiences, planned with intention, are enough to leave a lasting mark.

One family set aside one Saturday a month for an outing. Sometimes it was a local park, other times a picnic by the river. The children still argued on the way, but by the end of the day they were laughing over a duck that stole bread or a race down the path. Weeks later, those stories resurfaced at dinner, retold with smiles instead of frustration.

Another family created "couch campouts" a few times a year. Everyone brought blankets, pillows, and snacks to the living room, where they watched a favorite film and fell asleep side by side. The novelty of sleeping outside their bedrooms made it feel like an adventure, and the kids began asking, "When's the next one?"

Memories also grow from annual traditions. A mother always snapped a family photo at the same spot on their summer hike, year after year. Looking back at the sequence of pictures became a reminder not just of growing taller, but of being together in that familiar place.

Ideas to make family memories stick:

- Backyard camping with flashlights and late-night stories.

- Bike rides that always end at the same ice cream shop.

- Seasonal traditions, like apple picking each fall or decorating cookies every winter.

- An annual "same spot" photo that becomes a time capsule of family life.

What lasts isn't who sat where at dinner or who fought over toys. It's the memory of being shoulder to shoulder on the couch, pedaling to the corner shop, or telling stories under the stars.

Chapter 10: Strategies To Take Care Of Yourself And Manage Stress As A Parent

"You cannot pour from an empty cup. Take care of yourself first."
— Unknown

I t happens in an instant. Your child ignores a simple request, and after hours of constant redirection, something inside you snaps. Your voice rises before you can stop it. Words come out sharper than you meant, and the room falls silent. Your child's eyes widen, and guilt washes over you almost immediately. You didn't want to yell, but the exhaustion left no room for patience. Later that night, as the house grows quiet, you replay the moment in your head and wonder how much more of this you can carry.

Many parents of children with ADHD know this cycle too well: the pressure builds, the outburst happens, and then the guilt sets in. The truth is, parenting a child with ADHD asks for more energy, patience, and flexibility than most people realize. Trying to give endlessly without replenishing yourself is like running on an empty tank—you can keep going for a while, but eventually the engine stalls.

Caring for yourself isn't selfish. It's a necessity. When you carve out time to rest, restore, and recharge, you're not abandoning your child; you're making sure you can show up for them in the way they need most. A calmer, steadier parent provides something no strategy or technique can replace: a sense of safety.

Picture a different moment. The same child is melting down over homework, but today you've had a short walk outside and a quiet cup of coffee earlier. Your breath feels steadier. You kneel down, keep your voice low, and guide them through the steps without raising your volume. The tension still exists, but the spiral doesn't take over. Your child senses your composure and calms faster, turning what could have been an explosive evening into a manageable challenge.

I once spoke with a father who worked long hours and came home drained every night. He admitted that his short temper often fueled clashes with his son. After making one change—protecting a half-hour walk for himself before returning home—he noticed a shift. He still faced the same challenges, but instead of snapping right away, he found himself listening longer and speaking more gently. Over time, his son's resistance softened too. Their evenings, once a series of battles, became less hostile and more cooperative. The only difference was that the father had begun to take care of himself.

That's the heart of this chapter. Your well-being is not separate from your parenting—it's part of it. When you are rested, nourished, and supported, you respond instead of react. You guide instead of explode. And that balance transforms the atmosphere in your home.

In the pages ahead, you'll find ten strategies designed specifically for you, the parent. These aren't abstract reminders to "relax more" or "find time for yourself." They are practical, doable steps that help reduce stress and preserve your energy—accepting the demands of ADHD parenting without letting them drain you dry. You'll learn how to acknowledge the difficulty without guilt, build a network of support, carve out real breaks, and even bring humor back into tense moments.

Every family is different, but the common thread is this: when you take care of yourself, you give your child a stronger version of you—the one who can handle challenges with patience, consistency, and love. By the end of this chapter, you'll have a toolkit to protect your own well-being, so that you can continue to guide your child with the strength they deserve.

Strategy 1: Accept That Parenting A Child With ADHD Is Demanding

There's a quiet relief in saying the words out loud: *"This is hard."* Too often, parents feel pressure to act as if everything is under control, even when inside they're running on empty. The gap between how you appear and how you actually feel only deepens frustration and shame.

When you deny the difficulty, guilt takes over. You might snap at your child and then hear that critical voice whisper, *"Other parents don't lose it like this. Maybe I'm not good enough."* The more you compare yourself to an impossible standard, the heavier the weight becomes.

Acceptance breaks that cycle. When you allow yourself to think, *"This is hard, and that's okay,"* you stop adding judgment on top of exhaustion. Naming the challenge doesn't make you weak—it makes you honest. And honesty clears space in your mind. Instead of fighting yourself, you can see your reality for what it is: demanding, yes, but not a reflection of failure.

One father described how he used to beat himself up every evening after yelling during homework time. He would replay the moment in his head, convinced that he was doing everything wrong. The shift came when he started saying quietly to himself, *"This was tough today. Anyone would feel stretched thin."* That sentence didn't solve the behavior issues, but it softened his inner critic. He noticed that when guilt loosened its grip, he could face the next day with a steadier outlook.

Acceptance doesn't erase the chaos, but it changes how you carry it. Instead of piling shame on top of struggle, you recognize the weight without blaming yourself for feeling it.

Acceptance reduces guilt and brings clarity.

Strategy 2: Build A Support Network Around You

Parenting a child with ADHD can often feel like standing in the middle of a storm with no umbrella. The intensity of daily life, with constant reminders, emotional outbursts and endless negotiations, can leave you drained before the day is even over. Trying to carry it all alone only multiplies that exhaustion.

The truth is, no parent is meant to do this work in isolation. A strong support network does not erase the challenges, but it lightens the load. When you have people who understand, listen, or step in when needed, the constant pressure softens.

Support can take many shapes:

- A grandparent who picks up your child from school once a week so you can rest.

- A neighbor who offers to host a short playdate, giving you a quiet hour.

- A friend who sends a message at the end of a hard day, reminding you that you are not alone.

- A cousin who organizes an afternoon outing with the kids, breaking the routine and giving you space to breathe.

- Parent groups, online or in person, where you can share struggles and hear ideas that come from lived experience.

One mother described how much strength she found in a small online group for parents of children with ADHD. At first she only read other posts, relieved to see her own struggles reflected back. Over time, she began sharing her experiences and asking questions. The responses she received were not from experts but from parents who knew the same exhaustion, and that solidarity gave her energy to keep going.

Professionals can also play a role in your circle, but they are only one part of a larger web. The heart of support lies in the people who stand beside you in everyday life, offering presence, encouragement, and practical relief.

Support makes the load lighter.

Strategy 3: Schedule Regular Breaks For Yourself

When every day is filled with the demands of parenting a child with ADHD, your own needs can quietly disappear. You keep pushing through, telling yourself you will rest later, but "later" rarely comes. The result is that by the time your child is finally in bed, you are too depleted to recharge in any meaningful way.

Breaks are not luxuries. They are the pauses that keep you from burning out. Even short ones can reset your body and mind so you return with more patience and perspective. Think of them as pressure valves that release stress before it builds too high.

These pauses are about time, not technique. They do not require special skills or structured practices. A ten minute walk around the block, a quiet coffee on the balcony, or reading a few pages of a book can shift how the rest of the day feels. Longer breaks, like an afternoon off while your children stay with grandparents, add even more relief, but even micro-pauses matter.

One father admitted he often went weeks without a moment to himself. He began setting aside ten minutes each evening after dinner. During that time, he stepped outside with no phone, no chores, just a short walk. He noticed that when he came back, he had more patience for the bedtime routine. It was not the length of the break that mattered, but the consistency.

Another mother arranged with a close friend to trade childcare once a month. Each took the other's children for an afternoon. That exchange gave both parents a chance to breathe without guilt, knowing their kids were cared for. She returned home lighter, able to handle the usual chaos with more calm. The benefit here was not in "building a network" but in creating space for herself.

The point is not when or how you take the break, but that it happens regularly. Protect those pauses the way you would a doctor's appointment. They are part of staying healthy enough to parent with clarity and steadiness.

Breaks prevent burnout before it starts, especially when they become a steady habit rather than a rare exception.

Strategy 4: Practice Stress Reduction Techniques Daily

Parenting a child with ADHD brings constant demands on your attention and patience. Even in quieter moments, the tension often lingers in your body—tight shoulders, shallow breathing, a mind that never switches off. Without tools to ease that pressure, stress accumulates until the smallest spark ignites a big reaction.

Stress reduction techniques are like quick resets. They do not require long breaks or special equipment, only small practices you can use right where you are. The aim is not to erase stress, but to keep it from running unchecked.

Some simple methods include:

- Deep breathing: inhaling slowly through the nose, then exhaling fully through the mouth. Even three rounds can lower your heart rate.

- Gentle stretching: rolling your shoulders or standing up to release tension in your back and neck.

- Mindful pauses: focusing on one sensory detail—the sound of water running, the feel of your feet on the floor—just for a minute.

- Calming audio: listening to soft music or a short guided meditation to shift your state of mind.

One mother began taking five slow breaths before answering her son when he shouted. At first it felt forced, but she noticed her voice stayed steadier. That single adjustment helped her son calm faster too, because he was responding to her composure instead of her frustration.

These practices work best when they are woven into everyday transitions: before starting dinner, while sitting in the car, or during a pause at your desk. They do not add extra tasks to your schedule—they blend into what you are already doing.

Calm parents create calmer homes, and the calm comes from micro-actions repeated daily that steadily lower the background noise of stress.

Strategy 5: Protect Your Sleep As A Parent

Exhaustion can turn even the smallest parenting challenge into a mountain. When you are running on too little rest, patience disappears quickly, and stress feels heavier than it really is. Many parents sacrifice their own sleep to catch up on chores, scroll on their phones, or carve out late-night "quiet time," but the cost shows up the next day in irritability and burnout.

This strategy is not about your child's bedtime routines. It is about your own. Protecting your sleep is one of the most effective ways to keep your reactions steady and preserve emotional balance. Children with ADHD need a regulated parent, and you can only provide that when your body and mind have had the chance to recover.

What makes the difference is structure:

- Set a consistent bedtime and wake-up time, even on weekends.

- Put away screens at least 30 minutes before bed to avoid overstimulation.

- Keep the bedroom clear of clutter so it signals rest, not unfinished tasks.

One father noticed that after years of staying up past midnight, his patience was paper-thin by morning. When he committed to going to bed an hour earlier and cutting out late-night phone use, the change was striking. Within a week, he felt sharper and less reactive with his children. Another parent realized she slept better simply by moving laundry baskets and toys out of the bedroom—removing visible reminders of chores made the space feel like a refuge.

This is not about quick pauses or calming exercises, which have their own place. Sleep protection is about building a reliable rhythm that restores you fully each night. Without it, you are running on fumes; with it, you give yourself the reserves to meet daily challenges without snapping.

Rested parents handle stress with more stability and emotional steadiness.

Strategy 6: Maintain A Balanced Diet And Exercise Routine For Yourself

When your meals are irregular and movement is scarce, stress weighs more heavily. Parenting a child with ADHD demands energy and steadiness, yet many parents cut corners on their own health. Over time, this neglect doesn't just tire your body; it chips away at patience and clarity.

Caring for yourself physically does not mean chasing a strict fitness plan. It means giving your body the fuel and activity it needs to support your mind through demanding days. Food stabilizes mood and energy, while movement helps release the tension that builds from constant responsibility.

Small adjustments make the difference:

- Replace a skipped lunch with a simple balanced plate, like yogurt with fruit and nuts.

- Keep a bottle of water nearby to stay hydrated instead of relying only on coffee.

- Take a twenty minute walk while your child is at practice or use the time to move your body in your own space.

- Fit activity into the household flow: stretch while waiting for the washing machine to finish, or take a few minutes for squats or stretches in the kitchen while dinner simmers.

One mother realized she often ate only scraps left over from her children's plates. Preparing a quick wrap just for herself at midday gave her energy that lasted through homework time, and she noticed she snapped less often in the evenings. A father who restarted light jogging twice a week found he didn't just feel physically stronger; he handled tantrums with more patience and made calmer choices in stressful moments.

This strategy is not about achieving perfection. It is about building a physical foundation that allows you to stay present when challenges appear.

Healthy nutrition and regular movement give you the patience to face conflicts and the clarity to make decisions without impulsive reactions.

Strategy 7: Use Humor To Release Tension

Life with ADHD can fill a house with noise, mess, and endless negotiations. When stress is high, it is easy for every mishap to feel like another battle. Humor can shift that energy in seconds. A laugh does not solve the problem, but it changes the atmosphere enough to make it manageable.

Humor works because it lowers tension for both you and your child. Smiles relax the body, soften voices, and reset the mood. The key is not to laugh at your child but to bring lightness into the moment you are both stuck in.

Examples of how parents use humor to ease daily stress:

- Playing a silly song when the living room is in chaos, turning frustration into a mini dance break.

- Pretending to give a mock "award" for the biggest pile of laundry instead of sighing at the mess.

- Making an exaggerated joke when milk spills, showing your child that mistakes do not always need drama.

- Laughing together at a funny face in the mirror before restarting a tough routine.

- Turning a traffic jam into a "sing-along contest" in the car, or joking about who can spot the silliest item during grocery shopping.

One father recalled a dinner where his son knocked over a glass of water for the third time that week. Instead of snapping, he raised his fork and declared, "We have a new family record!" Everyone laughed, and the tension evaporated. Cleaning up was still necessary, but the mood had shifted from anger to cooperation.

Humor is not a pause or a relaxation technique. It is an active way of steering the atmosphere in real time, keeping situations from spiraling and helping your child follow your lead.

Laughter is a stress reliever you can use anytime, and it keeps you in the role of a calm, approachable guide even when the day feels overwhelming.

Strategy 8: Set Boundaries With Extended Family And Friends

Parenting a child with ADHD often brings a flood of opinions. Relatives may call for stricter discipline, friends may draw comparisons, and neighbors might make comments in public. Even when well meant, these voices can feel overwhelming and leave you doubting your own judgment. Clear boundaries protect your peace of mind and allow you to stay focused on your child.

A boundary is a way of steering conversations and interactions so they support rather than drain you. Short and respectful responses prevent debates from escalating. Choosing which topics are off-limits helps you keep control.

Here are practical ways to set boundaries:

- Prepare neutral phrases such as "We are working on this with our therapist, thank you" or "This approach works for our family."

- Decide in advance which areas are not open for discussion, such as medication or discipline methods.

- Limit time with people who leave you feeling judged or exhausted.

- Spend more time with relatives and friends who offer encouragement and respect your choices.

One mother described how her parents often questioned her handling of her son's outbursts. Every visit left her frustrated. She began repeating calmly, "We have a plan in place, and we are following it." At first it felt uncomfortable, but over time the comments slowed and the pressure eased. That boundary freed her to focus on her son instead of defending herself.

Boundaries may take practice, but they build respect. By being clear and consistent, you shape how others treat you and create an environment where your family can breathe.

Strategy 9: Pursue Personal Interests Outside Parenting

When parenting takes up every corner of your identity, stress grows heavier. Days revolve around meals, homework, meltdowns, and appointments until it feels like there is no space left for the person you were before becoming a parent. Over time, that loss of self makes you more irritable and less resilient.

Keeping a piece of your own life alive is not selfish. It is a way to preserve your sense of identity and bring more patience back into your role as a parent. Personal interests remind you that you are more than the responsibilities you carry. They give you joy that is separate from the daily challenges of ADHD.

These interests do not have to be grand. They simply need to be yours:

- Reading a book you choose for yourself, not related to parenting.

- Joining a weekly dance or cooking class.

- Tending a garden or caring for plants on the balcony.

- Practicing a musical instrument you once enjoyed.

- Participating in a book club or helping at a small local volunteer group.

One mother decided to dedicate one evening a week to a community dance class. At first she felt guilty leaving her children with her partner, but she soon realized that the hour of movement and laughter changed how she approached the rest of the week. She came home calmer, lighter, and more willing to handle the bedtime chaos.

Another parent found joy in a simple routine of early morning reading. Just fifteen minutes with a novel before the house woke up gave her something to look forward to and helped her start the day with a clearer mind.

The size of the interest is not what matters. What matters is keeping a part of yourself alive that has nothing to do with parenting. That personal corner becomes a well you can draw from when family life feels overwhelming.

When you keep a personal interest alive, you return to your children with more energy and less irritability.

Strategy 10: Seek Professional Help When Needed

Parenting a child with ADHD can sometimes feel like carrying a weight that no amount of friendly advice or family support can lift. Relatives and peers may offer encouragement, but there are moments when the challenges call for tools that only trained professionals can provide. Reaching out for that kind of help is not a failure. It is a deliberate step toward stability.

Professional guidance creates a safe space where you can talk about your struggles without fear of judgment. A therapist, counselor, or coach brings structured strategies tailored to your situation, helping you manage stress in ways that informal support networks cannot. Even short consultations can change how you approach overwhelming moments.

Examples of how parents have used professional help include:

- A mother who began individual therapy to confront her guilt and learned to separate her self-worth from her child's behavior.

- A father who joined family counseling sessions, where both parents practiced consistent ways of responding to meltdowns.

- A parent who found new confidence in a support group led by a trained facilitator, discovering practical approaches alongside other families.

- Another who scheduled a brief consultation with the school psychologist, gaining concrete tips on structuring afternoons at home.

These professionals do not take away your role as a parent. They give you tools that strengthen your resilience and preserve the stability of your household. Just as you would seek medical care for a physical condition, you can seek emotional and psychological care when the weight of parenting feels too heavy.

Asking for help is a sign of strength, and it protects both your well-being and the balance of your family.

A Note Before You Go

Parents who support each other create ripples that reach far beyond their own homes. A few words of feedback may seem small, but they can be the difference between another parent giving up or trying again. Would you take a brief moment to share your honest thoughts? It costs nothing and doesn't need to be long, yet the impact lasts.

Your review can help:

• a parent feel less alone

• a child benefit from practical strategies

• a family see that their struggles are shared

I read every review, positive or critical, and value them all. If these pages offered you a tool, a new perspective, or a bit of relief, consider taking that short step. It may be the encouragement another family needs.

Scan to leave a review on Amazon

Thank you for being part of this effort.

— Talia

Conclusion

"Do what you can, with what you have, where you are." —
Theodore Roosevelt

Y ou've carried a lot to make it this far. Not just through these pages, but through the long days and nights that made you reach for them in the first place.

Nothing about your child—or about you—needs to be torn down and rebuilt. The strength you need is already there. What changes is how you use it, where you place your energy, and which moments you decide to meet with calm instead of conflict.

ADHD will still be present tomorrow. There will still be mornings that unravel and evenings that stretch your patience. But now you can approach those moments differently. Not with perfection, not every time, but with enough steadiness to see that you are not powerless, and neither is your child.

The changes you'll notice rarely arrive in a dramatic way. They show up quietly: a morning that feels lighter than usual, a bedtime that ends without shouting, a laugh you didn't expect after a long day. These small shifts are proof that life can bend toward something easier to carry.

This book doesn't need to follow you every day. Close it when you want to. Come back only if you need a reminder, or if a new challenge asks for another idea. The rest belongs to you.

Parenting a child with ADHD isn't about chasing flawless routines or perfect discipline. It's about moving forward, again and again, with the strength you already hold. Hold on to that. It's enough.

Bibliography

- Lee, P.-C., Niew, W.-N., Yang, H.-J., Chen, V. C. H., & Lin, K.-C. (2012). A meta-analysis of behavioral parent training for children with attention-deficit hyperactivity disorder. *Research in Developmental Disabilities*, 33(6), 2040–2049.

- Zwi, M. (2011). Parent training interventions for Attention Deficit Hyperactivity Disorder. *Cochrane Database of Systematic Reviews*, (12), CD003018.

- Doffer, D. P. A., Dekkers, T. J., Hornstra, R., van der Oord, S., Luman, M., Leijten, P., Hoekstra, P. J., van den Hoofdakker, B. J., & Groenman, A. P. (2023). Sustained improvements by behavioural parent training for children with attention-deficit/hyperactivity disorder: A meta-analytic review of longer-term child and parental outcomes. *JCPP Advances*, 3(3), e12196.

- Dekkers, T. J., Hornstra, R., van der Oord, S., Luman, M., Hoekstra, P. J., Groenman, A. P., & van den Hoofdakker, B. J. (2022). Which components of parent training work best across different clinical settings? A meta-analysis of behavioral parent training for ADHD. *Journal of the American Academy of Child & Adolescent Psychiatry*, 61(8), 1143–1155.

- van der Oord, S., & Tripp, G. (2020). How to improve behavioral parent and teacher training for children with ADHD: Integrating empirical research on learning and motivation into treatment. *Clinical Child and Family Psychology Review*, 23(4), 577–604.

- Paiva, G. C. C., et al. (2024). Parent training for disruptive behavior symptoms in children with ADHD and ODD: Effects on symptoms, positive parenting, and quality of life. *Frontiers in Psychology*, 15, Article 1293244.

- Piscitello, J. (2024). A randomized controlled trial of a virtually delivered group parent training for parents of children with ADHD during an intensive summer treatment program. *Journal of Attention Disorders*, in press.

- Helander, M., et al. (2024). The efficacy of parent management training with or without child CBT for disruptive behavior. *Child and Adolescent Mental Health*, 29(1), 15–25.

- Walcott, C. M., Carlson, J. S., & Beamon, H. L. (2009). Effectiveness of a self-administered parent training program for parents of children with ADHD. *School Psychology Forum: Research in Practice*, 9, 59–69.

- Dale, C. (2022). Behavioral parent training for preschool ADHD: Family-predictor study. *Journal of Clinical Child & Adolescent Psychology*, 51(5), 755–765.

- Lynch, J. D. (2025). Reinforcement processing as a predictor of behavioral intervention response in ADHD. *Behavior Therapy*, 56(2), 155–166.

- Lindström, T., et al. (2024). Development of the Improving Parenting Skills Adult ADHD (IPSA) Program. *Journal of Attention Disorders*, 28(4), 531–541.

- Rimestad, I., et al. (2019). Preschool ADHD long-term outcomes following behavioral parent training. *Journal of Child Psychology and Psychiatry*, 60(7), 743–751.

- Daley, D., et al. (2014). Behavioral interventions in ADHD: A meta-analysis across outcome domains. *Journal of the American Academy of Child & Adolescent Psychiatry*, 53(8), 835–847.

- Van Aar, J., Leijten, P., Orobio de Castro, B., & Overbeek, G. (2017). Sustained, fade-out or sleeper effects? A systematic review and meta-analysis of parenting interventions for disruptive child behavior. *Clinical Psychology Review*, 51, 153–163.

- Matos, M., Bauermeister, J. J., & Bernal, G. (2009). Parent-child interaction therapy for Puerto Rican preschool children with ADHD and behavior problems: A pilot efficacy study. *Family Process*, 48(2), 232–252.

- Lange, A.-M., et al. (2018). Preschool ADHD in routine specialist care: A randomized controlled trial. *Journal of the American Academy of Child & Adolescent Psychiatry*, 57(8), 593–602.

- van den Hoofdakker, B. J., et al. (2007). Effectiveness of behavioral parent training for children with ADHD in routine clinical practice: A randomized controlled study. *Journal of the American Academy of Child & Adolescent Psychiatry*, 46(10), 1263–1271.

- Barkley, R. A. (2002). Psychosocial treatments for ADHD in children. *Journal of Clinical Psychiatry*, 63(Suppl 12), 36–43.

- Williford, A. P., & Shelton, T. L. (2014). Behavior management for preschool-aged children. *Child and Adolescent Psychiatric Clinics of North America*, 23(4), 717–730.

- McKee, T. E., et al. (2004). Parental coping and parent–child interactions in ADHD. *Journal of Clinical Child and Adolescent Psychology*, 33(1), 158–168.

- Barkley, R. A. (1997). Behavioral inhibition, sustained attention, and executive functions: Constructing a unifying theory of ADHD. *Psychological Bulletin*, 121(1), 65–94.

- Faraone, S. V., et al. (2002). Genetics of ADHD: What a clinician should know. *Current Psychiatry Reports*, 4(1), 40–45.

- Sonuga-Barke, E. J. S., et al. (2013). Nonpharmacological interventions for preschoolers with ADHD. *American Journal of Psychiatry*, 170(3), 239–250.

- Storebø, O. J., et al. (2019). Social skills training for ADHD in children: Cochrane Review. *Cochrane Database of Systematic Reviews*, (6), CD010583.

- Westwood, S. J., Parlatini, V., Rubia, K., Cortese, S., & Sonuga-Barke, E. J. S. (2023). Computerized cognitive training in ADHD: Meta-analysis of RCTs. *Molecular Psychiatry*, 28(4), 1809–1820.

- Peterson, B. S., et al. (2024). Treatments for ADHD in children and adolescents: A systematic review. *Pediatrics*, 154(4), e2022057573.

- Wolraich, M., Hagan, J. F. Jr., Allan, C., et al. (2019). Clinical practice guideline for ADHD diagnosis and treatment. *Pediatrics*, 144(4), e20192528.

- Kazdin, A. E. (2005). Parent management training: Treatment for oppositional and antisocial behavior. *Journal of the American Academy of Child & Adolescent Psychiatry*, 44(7), 592–605.

- Furlong, M., McGilloway, S., Bywater, T., Hutchings, J., & Smith, S. M. (2013). Group-based parenting programmes for conduct problems: Meta-analysis. *Behaviour Therapy*, 44(3), 398–415.

- Sonuga-Barke, E. J. S., Brandeis, D., Cortese, S., Daley, D., & Ferrin, M. (2014). Computer-based cognitive training for ADHD: Review. *Child and Adolescent Psychiatric Clinics of North America*, 23(4), 807–825.

- Mechler, K., Banaschewski, T., Hohmann, S., & Häge, A. (2022). Evidence-based pharmacological treatment options for ADHD in children. *Pharmacology & Therapeutics*, 241, 108109.

- Faraone, S. V., & Glatt, S. J. (2010). A comparison of the efficacy of medications for ADHD: A meta-analysis. *Journal of Clinical Psychiatry*, 71(6), 754–763.

- Sonuga-Barke, E. J. S., et al. (2023). Hyperfocus symptoms and internet addiction in ADHD traits. *Frontiers in Psychiatry*, 14, 784310.

- Leclercq, S., Bleazard, R., & Renisley, M. (2025). The aetiology of ADHD: A systematic review. *European Neuropsychopharmacology*, 42, 35–48.

- Grimm, O., Kranz, T. M., & Reif, A. (2020). Genetics of ADHD: What clinicians need to know. *Current Psychiatry Reports*, 22(2), 7.

- Kuo, P. L., et al. (2024). Long-term outcomes of interventions for ADHD: Systematic review. *Psychology Research and Behavior Management*, 17, 299–319.

- Peterson, B. S., Trampush, J., Maglione, M., Bolshakova, M., & Rozelle, M. (2024). ADHD diagnosis and treatment in children and adolescents. *AHRQ Comparative Effectiveness Reviews*, 257, 1–198.

- Sonuga-Barke, E. J. S., et al. (2013). Nonpharmacological treatments in ADHD: Meta-analysis. *American Journal of Psychiatry*, 170(3), 239–250.

- Newcorn, J. H. (2000). The MTA study results: Behavior therapy plus medication. *Current Psychiatry Reports*, 2(2), 120–125.

- Peterson, B. S., et al. (2019). Long-acting stimulant and non-stimulant medication review. *American Journal of Managed Care*, 25(7), e216–e225.

- Bader, A., & Adesman, A. (2012). Complementary and alternative therapies for ADHD. *Current Opinion in Pediatrics*, 24(6), 652–658.

- Sekiyama, T. (2023). EEG biofeedback impact on ERPs in ADHD. *Journal of Neurotherapy*, 25(1), 1–12.

- Lin, L., Li, N., & Zhao, S. (2025). Effect of intelligent monitoring of physical exercise on executive function in ADHD children. *Developmental Neuropsychology*, 50(4), 355–368.

- Richter, B., Petras, I.-K., Vollmer, A.-L., Luong, A., Siniatchkin, M., & Wrede, B. (2024). VACO: Virtual robotic agent for concentration in ADHD. *International Journal of Human-Computer Studies*, 170, 102918.

- Storebø, O. J., et al. (2013). Parent management training for disruptive behavior: Real-world effectiveness review. *Clinical Child and Family Psychology Review*, 16(3), 218–230.

- Kazdin, A. E. (2014). Is parenting the mediator of change in BPT for externalizing problems? *Clinical Psychology Review*, 34(8), 757–767.

- Webster-Stratton, C., Hollinsworth, T., & Kolpacoff, M. (1989). The "Incredible Years" training series: Parents and children interventions. *Journal of Clinical Child Psychology*, 18(1), 20–29.

- Webster-Stratton, C. (2002). The Incredible Years®: Parents, Teachers, and Children Training Series. *Research in Developmental Disabilities*, 23(1), 17–32.

- Chronis-Tuscano, A., et al. (2011). Parent ADHD and evidence-based treatment outcomes for their children. *Journal of Consulting and Clinical Psychology*, 79(4), 477–487.

www.ingramcontent.com/pod-product-compliance
Lightning Source LLC
Chambersburg PA
CBHW072154270326
41930CB00011B/2424